Princess
& The Hustler

by
CHINONYEREM ODIMBA

Princess & The Hustler was first produced as a co-production between Eclipse Theatre Company, Bristol Old Vic and Hull Truck Theatre. It premiered at Bristol Old Vic on 9 February 2019, followed by a UK tour visiting seven cities.

FOREWORD

I started Revolution Mix, an Eclipse movement, to challenge the fact that most Black stories in British theatre, film and radio were either imported or were the stories of new arrivals. I wanted to empower Black British artists to tell our stories. In 2015, conscious of a pervading erasure of Black British stories, I worked with a group of writers researching five centuries of this untapped vein of British history. This was the jumping off point for the development of Revolution Mix – our aim to produce the largest body of new Black British work in theatre, film and radio.

The first production – *Black Men Walking* – is an epic walk across the Peaks that uncovers two thousand years of hidden Black Yorkshire histories. Inspired by a real walking group, it had a sold-out UK tour. *The Last Flag* (BBC Radio 4, Afternoon Play) is set in an imagined near-future world where identity and empathy are electronically controlled.

Princess & The Hustler is a more recent but equally forgotten story from Bristol. This 1963 story is a domestic drama set in the home of a black family that cleverly combines the politics of colourism with The Bristol Bus Boycott – a seminal Black British civil rights action that led to the Race Relations Act of 1965. *Princess & The Hustler* is a story of Black agency that is funny, powerful and uplifting.

This production will be the first time that Eclipse has worked with a community chorus – made up of local audiences who will appear onstage alongside our incredible cast. It is exciting that Revolution Mix audiences are not only the inspiration for our work but now can participate. Onwards.

Dawn Walton
Artistic Director – Eclipse

Princess
& The Hustler
by CHINONYEREM ODIMBA

CAST

Phyllis 'Princess' James   Kudzai Sitima
Mavis James   Donna Berlin
Wendell 'Junior'   Fode Simbo
Wendell 'The Hustler' James   Seun Shote
Lorna James   Emily Burnett
Margot   Jade Yourell
Leon   Romayne Andrews

CREATIVE TEAM

Director   Dawn Walton
Designer   Simon Kenny
Lighting Designer   Aideen Malone
Composer and Sound Designer   Richard Hammarton
Movement Director   Victoria Igbokwe
Fight Director   Stephen Medlin
Voice and Dialect Coach   Joel Trill
Assistant Director   Emilie Lahouel
Dramaturg   Ola Animashawun
Casting Director   Briony Barnett

Producer   Ros Terry
Production Manager   Mark Carey
Company Stage Manager   Helen Drew
Deputy Stage Manager   Jane Williamson
Assistant Stage Manager   Sophie Keers
Wardrobe Supervisor   Emma Cains
Wig Supervisor   Sid Kennedy
Tour Technician   Jake Channon

CAST

KUDZAI SITIMA | PHYLLIS 'PRINCESS' JAMES
Kudzai Sitima is a Zimbabwean-British actress-singer-songwriter, who trained at Rose Bruford College.

Theatre credits include: *Sonnet Sunday* (Shakespeare's Globe); *random/generations* (Chichester Minerva Theatre); *An Introduction to Clean Love*, *Goldoni's Holiday Trilogy*, *Guernica*, *The River* (Rose Bruford) and *Not Bound Within* (Tristan Bates Theatre).

DONNA BERLIN | MAVIS JAMES
Donna Berlin is an actress, dancer, choreographer and movement director. She started dancing at the age of three and her love of the performing arts grew when she later attended stage school. At the age of eleven she appeared in her first film – Pink Floyd's *The Wall* – and since then she has never looked back.

Theatre credits include: *The Chalk Garden* (Chichester Festival Theatre); *Great Apes* (Arcola Theatre); *Of Kith and Kin* (Sheffield Crucible/Bush Theatre); *Anna Karenina*, *Rolling Stone* (Royal Exchange Theatre/WYP); *Blood Wedding*, *The Bacchae* (Royal & Derngate Theatre); *Keeping Mum* (Brockley Jack Theatre); *Counted/Look Right Look Left* (County Hall/UK tour); *Elmina's Kitchen* (UK tour/Garrick Theatre); *Puffins* (nabokov/Southwark Playhouse) and *The Vagina Monologues* (Pleasance Theatre, London).

Television credits include: *Requiem*, *Game Face*, *EastEnders*, *Todd Margaret*, *Coronation Street*, *Hollyoaks*, *New Tricks*, *Extras* – Series B, *Lead Balloon*, *Casualty*, *Doctors*, *Judge John Deed* and *Beautiful People*.

Film credits include: *In Darkness*, *Monochrome*, *Dinner With My Sisters*, *Press Your Lips* (LFS short); *Blinda* (short).

FODE SIMBO | WENDELL 'JUNIOR' JAMES
Fode Simbo trained at Guildhall School of Music and Drama.

Theatre credits include: *Young Marx* (Bridge Theatre); *Notoriously Abused*, *Crazy for You*, *Balm In Gilead*, *Herons*, *Great Expectations* and *The Crucible* (Guildhall).

Television credits include: *Summer of Rockets*, *Little Women* (BBC) and *Electric Dreams: Philip K Dick/Human Is* (Channel 4).

SEUN SHOTE | WENDELL 'THE HUSTLER' JAMES

Seun Shote is a creative and versatile actor who trained at Manchester Metropolitan University Acting Academy.

Theatre credits include: *Pitchfork Disney* (Jamie Lloyd Productions); *Play Mas* (Orange Tree Theatre, Richmond; nominated for an Offie for Best Actor 2015); *Routes* (Royal Court Theatre); *One Man, Two Guvnors* (National Theatre/international tour); *Death and the King's Horseman* (National Theatre) and *Salome* (Headlong).

Television credits include: *Black Mirror* (Netflix); *Creeped Out* (CBBC); *Unforgotten* (ITV); *Birds of a Feather, One Child, Little Miss Jocelyn* (BBC) and *Skins* (Channel 4).

Film credits include: *Bruno* (dir. Karl Golden); *Welcome to the Punch* (Momentum Films); *Farming* (Farming the Film Ltd); *Life and Lyrics* (Tailor Made Films); *Les Oiseaux Du Ciel* (Autonomous Films) and *Above* (Film London).

EMILY BURNETT | LORNA JAMES

Emily Burnett has recently filmed *The Buzz* for BBC WALES, *Warren* for BBC1 and *Merched Parchus* for S4C. You can currently see Emily in CBBC's *The Dumping Ground.*

Theatre credits include: Smart Simone in *Jack and the Beanstalk* (Oxford Playhouse); Gerda in *The Snow Queen* (Bristol Old Vic); My Only Girl in *Karagula* (DEM Productions/Soho Theatre); Skye in *Beacons* (Park Theatre); Rdeca in *First Love is the Revolution* (Soho Theatre); Pinocchio in *Pinocchio* (Midsummer Festival Company); Fairy in *Lolanthe* (Concept Players) and Mina in *Unga Bunga* (Stage Daze).

Television credits include: *The Dumping Ground* (CBBC); Safiya in *It's My Shout* (BBC Wales); Charlie in *Sweet Sixteen/It's My Shout* (BBC Wales) and *The Sparticle Mystery* (CBBC).

JADE YOURELL | MARGOT

Jade Yourell is an Irish actress and voice-over artist who has worked with some of Ireland's most influential and innovative directors for stage and screen. Jade was nominated for the IFTA (Irish Film and Television Award) for Best Actress in a Leading Role thanks to her memorable role in *Happy Ever Afters*.

Theatre credits include: *Absolute Hell*, *The Red Barn* (National Theatre); *Country Girls* (Chichester Festival Theatre); *Translations* (Millennium Forum); *Arcadia*, *Hayfever*, *Celebration*, *Present Laughter*, *Salome*, *Festen*, *The Constant Wife*, *That Was Then*, *The Importance of Being Earnest*, *An Ideal Husband* (The Gate).

TV credits include: *Guilt* (ABC); *Penny Dreadful* (Showtime); *Vexed*, *Doctors* (BBC); *Raw*, *Fair City* (RTÉ).

Film credits include: *All is By My Side* (dir. John Ridley); *The Food Guide to Love* (dir. Dominic Harari); *The Fairy Flag* (dir. David Izatt); *Happy Ever After* (dir. Stephen Burke) and *Waiting for Dublin* (dir. Roger Tucker).

ROMAYNE ANDREWS | LEON

Romayne Andrews trained at the Mountview Academy of Theatre Arts, graduating in 2014. Theatre whilst training included Antipholus of Syracuse in *The Comedy of Errors* and roles in *Macbeth* and *Richard III*.

Theatre credits include: *Hamlet*, *King Lear*, *Cymbeline* (RSC); *A Fox on the Fairway* (Queen's Theatre, Hornchurch); *The Country Girls* (Chichester Festival Theatre); *Richard III* (West Yorkshire Playhouse) and *Unearthed*, *The Gift*, *Larksong* (New Vic Theatre, Stoke).

Television credits include: *Doctors* (BBC).

CREATIVE TEAM

CHINONYEREM ODIMBA | WRITER

Chinonyerem Odimba is a Nigerian-born playwright and poet. Her work includes *The Bird Woman of Lewisham* at the Arcola; *Rainy Season* and *His Name is Ishmael* for Bristol Old Vic; *Joanne* for Clean Break, *Amongst the Reeds* for Clean Break and The Yard; *Medea* at Bristol Old Vic; *We Too, Are Giants* for Kiln Theatre; *Scotch Bonnet* for BBC Three and *A Blues for Nia* for the BBC and Eclipse Theatre. She is the winner of the 2018 Sonia Friedman Award.

Chino's first radio play *The Last Flag*, an Eclipse production co-written with Selina Thompson and Lorna French, was broadcast on BBC Radio 4 in May 2018, and was named Radio Drama of the Week. Having recently finished work on *Princess & The Hustler*, she is working on a new community play at Kiln Theatre. She is currently Writer-in-Residence at Live Theatre/Northumbria University.

DAWN WALTON | DIRECTOR

For Eclipse Theatre, credits include: *Black Men Walking* (shortlisted for the UK Theatre Best New Play and nominated for Writers' Guild Best Play 2019); *A Raisin in the Sun* (UK Theatre Best Touring Production nomination); *One Monkey Don't Stop No Show*, *The Hounding of David Oluwale* (TMA: Best Director nomination). Other theatre credits include: *Oxford Street* (Olivier Awards nomination); *93.2fm* (Royal Court Theatre); *Winners, The Blacks* (Young Vic); *There's Only One Wayne Matthews* (Sheffield Theatres); *Lyrikal Fearta* (Sadler's Wells) and *Urban Legend* (Liverpool Everyman).

Radio credits include: *The Last Flag* (BBC Radio 4; Radio Drama of the Week).

Film: for Eclipse, produced and directed *10by10*, a series of ten short film dramas now a featured collection on Digital Theatre Plus.

Other recent productions include: *salt.* (Selina Thompson Ltd; winner of The Stage Edinburgh Award; The Total Theatre Award for Experimentation, Innovation and Playing with Form; The Filipa Brangaca Award for Best Female Solo Performance).

SIMON KENNY | DESIGNER

Simon Kenny is a UK-based set and costume designer working in theatre, opera and live performance. He trained at the Central School of Speech and Drama.

Recent theatre credits include: *Noughts & Crosses* (Derby Theatre); *Cabaret* (English Theatre Frankfurt); *Macbeth* (Stafford Shakespeare Festival); *Le Nozze Di Figaro* (Nevill Holt Opera); *The Selfish Giant* (Vaudeville Theatre); *Sweeney Todd* (Harrington's Pie & Mash Shop, West End & Off-Broadway; nominated for the 2017 Drama Desk Award for Outstanding Set Design of a Musical); *Broken Glass* (Watford Palace Theatre); *Black Men Walking* (Eclipse/Royal Exchange Theatre/Royal Court Theatre); *Holes* (Nottingham Playhouse); *Wind in the Willows* (Sherman Theatre); *Peter Pan* (Mercury Theatre, Colchester); *Rose* (HOME); *Platinum* (Hampstead Theatre); *Babette's Feast* (The Print Room); *Twelfth Night* and *The Merchant of Venice* (Shakespeare's Globe).

AIDEEN MALONE | LIGHTING DESIGNER

Aideen Malone studied Drama and Theatre at Trinity College Dublin and Goldsmiths College, University of London.

Recent credits include: *The Worst Witch* (Royal & Derngate Theatre); *Darbar Festival* (Sadler's Wells); *Much Ado About Nothing* (Watford Palace Theatre); *A Monster Calls* (Old Vic/Bristol Old Vic); *Brighton Rock* (York Theatre Royal); *Napoleon Disrobed* (Told by an Idiot); *Raft* (GED); *La Strada* (Belgrade Theatre); *Jane Eyre* (National Theatre/Bristol Old Vic); *Fiddler on the Roof* (Liverpool Everyman); *Peter Pan* (National Theatre); *Conquest to the North Pole* (Liverpool Everyman); *Hetty Feather* (Duke of York's Theatre); *Frankenstein* (Living Spit); *Unkindest Cut* (Sadhana); *Time Over Distance Over Time* (Liz Roche); *Kaash (*Akram Kahn) and *A Raisin in the Sun* (Eclipse).

RICHARD HAMMARTON | COMPOSER AND SOUND DESIGNER

Richard Hammarton is a composer and sound designer for theatre, TV and film, his work has been heard throughout the UK and internationally. He was part of the design team that won the Manchester Evening News Best Design Award for *Dr Faustus* in 2010, and was Sound Designer for the Olivier Award-winning play, *The Mountaintop*. He also worked on the Ivor Novello-winning *Ripper Street* for TV.

Theatre credits include: *Under Milk Wood* (Northern Stage); *Women in Power* (Nuffield Theatre); *Describe the Night, Deposit* (Hampstead Theatre); *Out of Sight* (fanShen tour); *Jekyll and Hyde* (Touring Consortium Theatre Company); *Love from a Stranger* (Royal & Derngate Theatre); *In the Event of Moone Disaster* (Theatre503); *Trestle, Hanna, Orca* (Papatango); *Burning*

Doors (Belarus Free Theatre); *Girls* (HighTide); *The Weir* (English Touring Theatre); *As You Like It* (Theatre by the Lake); *Traitor* (Pilot Theatre); *Faust x2* (Watermill Theatre); *Dirty Great Love Story* (Arts Theatre); *Assata Taught Me* (Gate Theatre); *Low Level Panic* (Orange Tree Theatre, Richmond); *Luv* (Park Theatre); *Much Ado About Nothing* and *Jumpy* (Theatr Clwyd).

EMILIE LAHOUEL | ASSISTANT DIRECTOR
Emilie Lahouel is a physical-theatre artist based in Manchester, her practice is deeply rooted in interdisciplinary collaboration with a specialism in working across theatre and live music.

Theatre credits include: *Poezest* (Bloomsbury Theatre); Movement and Assistant Director on *Drift* (Lowry Theatre); Director and Producer on *Only Speak When Spoken To* (HOME/Lowry/CPT); Co-creator and Performer on *Millgirls and Militants* (Ludus Dance); Lead Artist on *Project X* (HOME; nominated for Manchester Cultural Award); Artist in Residence on *The Welcoming Party* (MIF/Theatre Rites); Associate Artist on *The Missy Elliott Project* (Selina Thompson LTD); Engagement Manager, Lead Artist and Co-producer and Performer on *Space Cassette* (Bluedot Festival).

OLA ANIMASHAWUN | DRAMATURG
As an actor, director, theatre-maker and writer, Ola Animashawun has been working in theatre for the past thirty years, with twenty of those years dedicated to specialising in script development as a dramaturg and facilitator. He is the co-founder and Creative Director of the playwriting consultancy, Euphoric Ink.

Ola is the National Theatre Connections Dramaturg, a former Associate Director of the Royal Court Theatre and founder of the Young Writers' Programme, and is also an Associate Artist, Dramaturg and Mentor for Belgrade Theatre, Theatre Absolute, Eclipse Theatre and the Royal Central School of Speech and Drama. He is also a patron of Graeae Theatre and Script Yorkshire.

BRIONY BARNETT | CASTING
Briony Barnett has worked in casting for over ten years in theatre, film and television.

Theatre credits include: *The Trick* (Bush Theatre/tour); *Again* (West End); *An Adventure* (Bush Theatre); *Abigail's Party* (Hull Truck); *Black Men Walking* (Royal Exchange Theatre/tour); *Female Parts* (Hoxton Hall); *Handbagged* (West End/Tricycle Theatre); *Fences* (West End/Theatre Royal Bath); *A Raisin in the Sun* (Sheffield Crucible/tour); *Ticking* (West

End); *Play Mas* (Orange Tree Theatre, Richmond); *The Invisible Hand, Ben Hur, A Wolf in Snakeskin Shoes, The House That Will Not Stand, The Colby Sisters* and *One Monkey Don't Stop No Show* (Tricycle Theatre).

Film credits include: *Bruce, Gypsy's Kiss, The Knot, High Tide, What We Did On Our Holiday* (children), *Common People, Tezz, Final Prayer, Love/Loss, Zero Sum* and *10by10*.

Television credits include: *Outnumbered* (children); *Just Around the Corner* (children); *Dickensian* (children) and *Inside the Mind of Leonardo*.

VICTORIA IGBOKWE | MOVEMENT DIRECTOR
Victoria Igbokwe is a creative director, choreographer and founder of Uchenna, a dance company based in London.

Creative director/choreographer credits include: *Our Mighty Groove* (UK tour); *The Head Wrap Diaries* (UK tour) and *Hansel & Gretel* (UK tour).

Movement director credits include: *The Woods* (Royal Court Theatre).

Mass movement choreographer credits include: London 2012 Olympic and Paralympic opening and closing ceremonies; Sochi 2014 Olympic and Paralympic opening and closing ceremonies; Glasgow 2014 Commonwealth Games opening ceremony; 2017 Islamic Solidarity Games opening and closing ceremonies.

Victoria is also a facilitator for The Fi.ELD 2019 (*Future Innovators East London Dance*), trustee for One Dance UK, and Associate Artist at The Place.

JOEL TRILL | VOICE AND DIALECT COACH
Having gained an MFA in Voice Studies, at the Royal Central School of Speech and Drama, Joel Trill now works as a voice coach in theatre and business training.

Theatre credits include: *good dog* (tiata fahodzi/Watford Palace Theatre); *The Wider Earth* (Natural History Museum); *Macbeth* (The Borgias Theatre); *Yellowman* (Young Vic); *Assata Taught Me* (Gate Theatre); *One Love* (Birmingham REP); *A Bitter Herb, Blues for an Alabama Sky* (RADA); *War & War* (Complicité/Pleasance Theatre); *Layla's Room, Rise Up* (The Theatre Centre) and *Clybourne Park* (RADA GBS studio).

Joel also works as a voice-over artist with clients that include: CNN, Sky Vision, Dreamwork's, Nike, BBC and ITV.

eclipse | **REVO LUTION MIX**

Eclipse Theatre

Artistic Director	Dawn Walton
Executive Director	Richard Oyarzabal
General Manager	Jonathan Ennis
Marketing Manager	Kelly France
Assistant Producer	Grace Lee

Slate Enablers
Deborah Baddoo – Slate Producer
Degna Stone
Adam Lowe
Chardine Taylor-Stone
Charlotte Bowen
Saphena Aziz

Audience Development Officers
Judith Davis
Siddi Majubah
Veronica Dewan
Curtis Watts
Beverley Prevatt Goldstein
Pat Green
Sadie McLaughin

Find out more
eclipsetheatre.org.uk
eclipsetcl / #PrincessAndTheHustler

PRINCESS & THE HUSTLER

Chinonyerem Odimba

With respect to:

Princess Campbell
Paul Stephenson
Roy Hackett
Guy Bailey
Raghbir Singh
Owen Henry
Joyce Stephenson
Carmen Beckford
Barbara Dettering
Audley Evans
Prince Brown
Mary Seacole
George Odlum
Mrs Mavis Bowen
Alfred Fagon
Clifford Drummond
Delores Campbell
Tony Benn
Tony Bullimore & Family
And many many more…

C.O.

People

PHYLLIS 'PRINCESS' JAMES, *ten years old*
MAVIS JAMES, *thirty-eight years old*
WENDELL 'JUNIOR' JAMES, *seventeen years old*
WENDELL 'THE HUSTLER' JAMES, *forty years old*
LORNA JAMES, *nine years old*
MARGOT, *forty-two years old*
LEON, *nineteen years old*

Places

1. Mavis's front room. A small front room with an even smaller
kitchenette in the corner of the room. Decorated sparsely with
pictures of the Caribbean and family members on the walls.
There is one small sofa and a dining table where a sewing
machine sits occasionally. A wireless radio sits on a small
mantelpiece.

2. Cupboard room. A large cupboard big enough to stand and
walk in – not big enough for a bed. This room is only lit when
Princess is in it.

3. The other room. The room Wendell Junior and Princess
share. Also becomes the room Wendell Junior shares with
Wendell.

4. The Docks, Bristol.

Things

…indicates a trailing off at the end of a sentence or a pause.

/ indicates an overlap in speech between two characters or within a character's dialogue.

A new paragraph indicates a natural pause/change of thought in dialogue.

VOICE-OVER – indicates pre-recorded news pieces.

This text went to press before the end of rehearsals and so may differ slightly from the play as performed.

ACT ONE

Scene One

Christmas Day. St Agnes, Bristol. 1962.

The stage opens like a big box – as though opening the front of a doll's house.

PRINCESS, *eyes closed, stands in the cupboard room.*
She is wearing a swimming costume and a sash around her.
She raises her hands in the air and places a crown made of cardboard and tinsel on her head.

VOICE-OVER. *Ladies and gentlemen, I present to you the winner of the year's Weston-super-Mare Beauties of the West Contest – (Voice booming.) Princess James.*

PRINCESS*'s eyes open wide.*
The cupboard room explodes into a world of pageantry – scenes of people jumping into a swimming pool, Union Jacks, music and fireworks – fill the stage.
PRINCESS *approaches a microphone.*

PRINCESS. My name is Phyllis Princess James. I will wear this crown every day. I will never take it off even when I am asleep.

I want to thank my mummy, my friends, Margot and Junior...

Even though he is so annoying!

I will use all this money to help the poor...

After I have bought my mummy a new coat and...

I might buy a new bicycle for me and...

MAVIS*'s voice can be heard shouting above the noise –*

MAVIS. Princess James did you hear what I said?

Princess!

If I have to carry on with this hollering at you then the next thing you hear will be my hand against your backside.

You hear me chile?

Phyllis!

PRINCESS *steps into the front room –*

PRINCESS *stands, crown on, sash falling off, dejected –*

PRINCESS. Mummy!

MAVIS. Don't you 'Mummy' me! Been calling you for the last ten minutes. Sometimes I do wonder where your head is at /

PRINCESS. Beauties of the West /

MAVIS. What you say?

PRINCESS. Nothing Mummy /

MAVIS. Good. Now go wash your hands and come help me with the beans. Not going to be eating until five o'clock if you children don't fix up.

Where's your brother?

Junior. Come here now.

Wendell Junior!

PRINCESS. I heard the door go this morning.

Or maybe I only think I hear it.

MAVIS. What you think you're saying?
You two thick as thieves in the night /

PRINCESS. I think I hear something...

The sound of footsteps heavy, climbing stairs –

WENDELL JUNIOR *enters.*
A camera swings around his neck –

*He casually walks across his mother and sister towards
another door –
He places his hand on the door handle –*

MAVIS. You turn the handle of that door and it will be the last
thing you do on this God-given earth.

WENDELL JUNIOR *releases his grip on the door handle –*

Beat.

I am done waiting for an explanation as to what reason you
might have for leaving this house this early today of all days.
You better having a conversation with the leather of the belt
instead.

MAVIS *moves to a cupboard. She opens it and pulls out
a man's leather belt –*

WENDELL JUNIOR. No! Mummy! Hold on a minute /

MAVIS. Oh you find the power of speech now?

WENDELL JUNIOR. It was some of the guys...

They were meeting up you know...
Gotta be there or be square!

MAVIS *flexes the belt –*

I should have told you but didn't want to wake you. I was
thinking better let you /

MAVIS. So you were doing it for me? Looking after your
mummy by sneaking out the house to Lord-knows-where at
Lord-knows-what-time for me. That right son?

PRINCESS. God doesn't go where he's been /

WENDELL JUNIOR. Shut your face!

PRINCESS. Mummy is going to beat you and you gone cry like
a baby.
Cry baby.

WENDELL JUNIOR *moves to grab at* PRINCESS –

WENDELL JUNIOR. If I beat you first then you gon' cry louder than me.

MAVIS *raises the belt high above her head* –

WENDELL JUNIOR *backs off* –

MAVIS. You done explaining yourself?

And now you have the nerve to be all sorts of cruel to your sister?

WENDELL JUNIOR. Mummy. I am really sorry.
We're doing nothing bad. We just hang by Queen Square with our cameras...

MAVIS. So let me get this right. You sneak out of my house at whatever time on this particular day to choose to go posing in the street /

WENDELL JUNIOR. Not posing Mummy.

Leon and some other guys wanted to take photographs by the docks. And you know I'm trying to learn everything I can...

I'll be an apprentice one day in one of them photography studios /

MAVIS. You're not an apprentice yet. Right now you are about to get another kind of education /

WENDELL JUNIOR. I split from those guys so I could come back and do portraits of you...

Mummy...

Gon' use some of my savings to get them developed in that place Leon goes. Over by Fishponds...

Going to take real pretty pictures of you.

MAVIS *puts down the belt* –

You gon' shine like a queen!

MAVIS *pats her hair* –

MAVIS. Pictures you say?

WENDELL JUNIOR. Yes Mummy. Right there in front of the…

> WENDELL JUNIOR *looks at the sad withering Christmas tree in the corner of the room –*

> MAVIS *shakes her head –*

By the wireless.
You just listening to the radio all casual like…
A movie star!
You going to wear your pearls?
They always make you look so ladylike.

> WENDELL JUNIOR *lifts the camera to his face, and circles his mother, pretending to be taking photos –*

MAVIS. You think so Junior?
Maybe…
You know when I iron out this wig and add a little colour on my face, you wouldn't even recognise your own mother.

> MAVIS *preens herself –*

PRINCESS. What about me? You going to take a photograph of me Junior?

WENDELL JUNIOR. No! Wasn't planning to break the glass of my new camera with your face.

> PRINCESS *bursts into heartbreaking sobs –*

> MAVIS *remembering the hundred and one things she still has to do, turns on her heels and heads for the small kitchenette –*

MAVIS. You stop that way of talking to your sister.

Princess you stop your noise and get started on those beans.

Junior you make sure you tidy up the bedroom, this room, and the washroom.

> WENDELL JUNIOR *stomps his foot in frustration –*

WENDELL JUNIOR. That is so uncool.

MAVIS. You got something else to say Junior?

WENDELL JUNIOR. No Mummy.

WENDELL JUNIOR *exits* –

PRINCESS. Mummy?

MAVIS *is busy at sink washing up* –

Mummy.

MAVIS. I hope when I turn round you're busy on those beans Princess. I just as easily pick that belt up again /

PRINCESS *busies herself with the pile of beans* –

PRINCESS. Doing it Mummy.

Doing it quicker even…

I need to ask you one question. Just one…

MAVIS. Go on then Princess.

PRINCESS. Why don't we have any presents under the tree?

MAVIS *turns to face* PRINCESS –

MAVIS. Nothing you really want beyond your family and this roast chicken I have in the oven.

PRINCESS. But they made me do the list at school. I was writing it in my best handwriting…

Even Miss Turner give me a gold star for how good my Gs and my Ys were /

MAVIS. Gave me /

PRINCESS. She said it was best in the class and '*considering my ability*' /

MAVIS. And what exactly is wrong with your ability?

MAVIS *kisses her teeth* –

I did read your list baby. I did. Every single word of it…

It's just…

Nobody ordering curtains at this time of year.

MAVIS *packs away the sewing machine –*

PRINCESS. Who needs presents all wrapped up in the sparkly paper and a pink ribbon? Who needs any of it?

When we have beans and pumpkin!

PRINCESS *bursts into a dance routine with the vegetables she is meant to be cutting up –*
MAVIS *starts to dance and laugh as she exits with the sewing machine.*

PRINCESS *is still doing her dance routine –*

WENDELL JUNIOR *enters.*

WENDELL JUNIOR. What you doing peahead?

PRINCESS. Mummy!

WENDELL JUNIOR *runs to put his hand over her mouth –*

PRINCESS *wriggles away from him –*

WENDELL JUNIOR. Why you always got to tell tales?

Princess you just need to grow up some time soon.
Most girls your age not so...

One day when you want to sneak out of the house /

PRINCESS. I am never going to be sneaking off to no place.
I am a good girl /

WENDELL JUNIOR. Course you are!

PRINCESS. And I'm big and grown enough /

WENDELL JUNIOR. Too big to still be dreaming of beauty pageants and crowns /

PRINCESS. Beauty pageants *are* for big girls.
Women. Grown girls and women.
Not little girls.
You know nothing Junior.

WENDELL JUNIOR. I know that if you tell tales on me again
I'm going to make sure you never get to Weston-super-Mare.
I'm going to tell Mummy about some of the ungodly things

that go on there. They say at night boys and girls go on the pier there to do sin. If I tell Mummy that then she will never let you go. Ever!

PRINCESS. You can't!

WENDELL JUNIOR. Then you better keep *that* shut /

PRINCESS. Margot says that they even give you free ice cream if you're really good. She is going to take me for my birthday. Margot says we can watch them all day. Watch all those women with perfect straight shiny hair all down to their waist /

WENDELL JUNIOR. Well none of that is going to happen when Mummy hears that Weston is worst than the devil's playground.
And Margot she says all sorts of things but none of them seem to ever happen so /

PRINCESS. I hate you Junior. I hate you and /

MAVIS *enters*.

MAVIS. We do not say such things in this house especially on *this* day.

PRINCESS. Junior was /

WENDELL JUNIOR *gestures a 'shush' at* PRINCESS *behind* MAVIS*'s back –*

Sorry Mummy.

PRINCESS *stomps off back to preparing the vegetables –*

WENDELL JUNIOR *slumps onto the small sofa –*

MAVIS. You tired son? You rest up. Put your feet up.
You want me to bring you a cold glass of something?
Or maybe put a blanket across your knees?

WENDELL JUNIOR. Thanks Mummy. Thinking of having a little shut-eye before food /

MAVIS *picks up a cushion and jokingly swipes* WENDELL JUNIOR *across the head –*

MAVIS. You wan ar lickle shut-eye is wha' ya say?

MAVIS *swipes at* WENDELL JUNIOR *with the cushion again –*

PRINCESS *giggles –*

Which food yuh gon' nyam?

Which table yuh gon' sit down 'pon?

PRINCESS *picks up another cushion and throws it at* WENDELL JUNIOR –

Yuh two children fool fool fram mawnin' till night!

PRINCESS *and* WENDELL JUNIOR *start to play/cushion fight –*

You watch yourselves and don't bring no mess to my house you hear me.

A loud knock at the door –

PRINCESS *and* WENDELL JUNIOR *don't hear the door –*

How many of them undercook mince pie I have to eat before these neighbours leave us alone?

MAVIS *walks to the door and opens it –*
She shuts the door quickly and goes back to clearing the table.

Scene Two

Ten minutes have passed. The knocking at the door is persistent now.

WENDELL JUNIOR *and* PRINCESS *are motionless, watching their mother. Watching the door.*

Beat.

PRINCESS. Mummy I think there's someone at the door /

WENDELL JUNIOR. You want me to get it? /

MAVIS. You stay where you are!

Beat.

Must be children from upstairs.

You see how they've been running up and down the street since morning like they don't have mothers. And what kind of mother let their children run wild like that.

Beat.

Princess you lay the table.

Another knock –

This chicken smells so good and the potatoes nearly done roasting.

WENDELL JUNIOR. You hear my belly?

MAVIS. Chile when you finished talking to your belly /

Knocking gets louder –

PRINCESS. Mummy /

MAVIS *wipes her hands on her apron –*

MAVIS. You make sure you lay those knives and forks straight and neat.

PRINCESS. Yes but Mummy /

WENDELL JUNIOR. One time when we at Deejay's house
the police came to ask him a few questions about some
business he say he never heard of. They come knocking in
this same way.

The police have anything to talk to you about Mummy?

PRINCESS. The police!

MAVIS. You lost your mind?

PRINCESS. They're going to take you away Mummy?

MAVIS. No one taking anyone any place!

MAVIS *turns to open the oven door –*

PRINCESS. I won't let them take you!

PRINCESS *stomps to the door, and before* MAVIS *can stop
her, she opens the door wide to reveal* WENDELL 'THE
HUSTLER' JAMES *standing tall and handsome on the
other side –*

MAVIS *and* WENDELL JUNIOR *freeze in shock –*

You can't take my mummy away! She hasn't done anything /

MAVIS. Move away from that door Princess!

WENDELL *bends down to face* PRINCESS –

WENDELL. Well hello Princess /

MAVIS. Now Princess!

PRINCESS *backs away from the door slowly – never taking
her eyes off* WENDELL –

WENDELL *straightens himself out –
Looks further into the room –*

MAVIS *gathers her children in her arms –*

WENDELL. Blouse an' skirt is dat Junior?

MAVIS *pushes them towards the door of the other room –*

MAVIS. You children go to your room /

> PRINCESS *and* WENDELL JUNIOR *remain still – frozen by curiosity –*

> You gone deaf? Your room now!

PRINCESS. Mummy.
  Do you know him?

MAVIS. You stop with the questions Princess /

WENDELL JUNIOR. You want me to stay?

WENDELL. An' hear dis! De bwoy gon' broke 'im voice.

> MAVIS *points at* WENDELL *– warning him –*

MAVIS. You / you…

> (*To her children.*) I won't tell you again /

PRINCESS (*groaning*). We haven't eaten our lunch yet.

> We haven't done Christmas /

> MAVIS *turns and slaps* PRINCESS *across the face –*

> PRINCESS *squeals and cools the stinging with her hand –*

> WENDELL JUNIOR *and* PRINCESS *exit.*

> MAVIS *stands staring at* WENDELL *–*

Scene Three

A few minutes have passed. WENDELL *moves further into the room.*

MAVIS *holds a cautionary hand out to stop him –*

WENDELL. Mavis /

MAVIS. No.

WENDELL. Lissen /

MAVIS. No.

WENDELL. I /

MAVIS. You /

WENDELL. Long time /

MAVIS. Ha! What kind of thing Satan bring to my door today. Unless you his ghost?

WENDELL. No.

MAVIS. Yes must be that /

WENDELL. It mi far real!!

MAVIS. No… No… No!

Take yourself fram mi house duppy.

WENDELL. Nuh be like dis Mavis.

Let mi juss come in an' tark…

Far ar lickle while…

Mi an' you…

Dat's all mi arsking.

MAVIS. If you don't take yourself out of my house, I will call the police on your backside.

WENDELL. Mavis mi know it ar shock.

Mi tink twice before mi come 'ere.

Tree times even. Mi tink real hard 'pon dis one.

Beat.

WENDELL *moves closer –*

MAVIS *walks to the kitchen, opens a drawer and pulls out a knife –*

WENDELL *backs off –*

Look at dis.

Let mi juss talk wit yuh ar lickle.

Juss ar lickle time far mi. Mi beg yuh Mavis.

MAVIS. Listen to me now Wendell. I don't have the time nor the inclination to abide your foolishness today.

If yuh nuh wan' to be lock up today, I beg you take yourself back to whatever ol' an' mess yuh juss crawl fram /

WENDELL. Yuh vex. Mi sees dat. Yuh vex in ar way an' yuh 'ave every right to be /

MAVIS. Vex? Vex? You come say *vex* like someone come and take my purse from my handbag.

Or eat too much from the Dutch pot.

Mi nuh *vex* Wendell. Mi beyon' vex.
Mi angry.
Mi angry nuff to kill yuh right 'ere an' den go tell yuh modder why.
Mi angry nuff to go to jail far dem years, an' still be laughing.

WENDELL. Tink of de children /

MAVIS *laughs out loud – hysterical – dangerous –*

MAVIS. Children?

MAVIS *waves the knife wildly –*

WENDELL. Wait wait /

MAVIS. Wait 'pon what?

We done talking now Wendell. You best step from mi door before I do something you going to regret /

WENDELL. De thing is Mavis /

MAVIS. Wendell mi nuh 'ave business wit you /

WENDELL. Mi kyaant go nuh place else /

MAVIS. Thank you for your visit.

WENDELL *backs out the door –*

You go duppy 'pon somebody else.

MAVIS *slams the door behind him –*

MAVIS *puts the knife away –*

Beat.

A knock at the door again –

Beat.

WENDELL. Mavis!!

Mavis.

You still mi wife yuh hear.

MAVIS *picks up the knife again and marches towards the door –*

MAVIS. Forgive me Father.

Mi gon' cut 'im rass throat!

MAVIS *jerks the door open –*
She lifts the knife up –

WENDELL *is standing at the door holding the hand of a girl barely younger than* PRINCESS –

MAVIS *lowers the knife slowly and hides it behind her back –*

Beat.

WENDELL. Mavis. Meet mi darter. Lorna.

Scene Four

Meanwhile…

WENDELL JUNIOR *and* PRINCESS *in the other room. It has two single beds – a small wardrobe against one wall and a small chair.*

WENDELL JUNIOR *is at the door – listening hard.*

PRINCESS *sits on one of the beds – face hardened – holding back tears.*

PRINCESS. Mummy hates me now doesn't she?

WENDELL JUNIOR. Princess…

PRINCESS. Junior…

WENDELL JUNIOR. Hush!

   WENDELL JUNIOR *goes back to listening at the door –*

PRINCESS. She hates me Junior. She hates me and she's going to give me away to the Salvation Army like them old jumpers from when I was a baby.

   PRINCESS *lets out a small sob –*

WENDELL JUNIOR. No one hates you Princess.

PRINCESS. But Mummy /

WENDELL JUNIOR. She didn't mean it.

   Beat.

   Is it still hurting? You want me to blow on it?

PRINCESS. No…

WENDELL JUNIOR. You want a lollipop?

   PRINCESS *nods –*

   WENDELL JUNIOR *hands her a bright-orange lollipop from his pocket –*

   PRINCESS *unwraps it eagerly and pops it into her mouth –*

PRINCESS. Junior?

What did I do that was so bad?

She looked meaner than the headteacher when she's walking down the corridor holding her ruler. She looked meaner than that…

WENDELL JUNIOR. She's trying to…

She wouldn't do it if she didn't have to…

Don't think she will again…

She only did it because she's needing to protect us /

PRINCESS. From what? She hit *me*! That's not protecting!

If I wasn't locked in here, I'd run away.

Next time I *am* going to have to run away. Sneak out in the night /

WENDELL JUNIOR. I told you! She didn't mean it…

She wouldn't if it wasn't because…

Try to grow up Princess. It's important because some things…

You're going to have to start understanding things different soon.

At that moment, the door is opened and LORNA *is shoved into the room –*
Door closes –

Beat.

PRINCESS. Hello.

LORNA. –

PRINCESS. My name is Princess.

What's your name?

LORNA. –

WENDELL JUNIOR. Sit down if you want.

LORNA *moves to sit on the other single bed –*

PRINCESS. That's Junior's bed. It smells of feet. Dirty feet and sweaty socks and –

LORNA *stands back up again –*

WENDELL JUNIOR. You see what you've done!

WENDELL JUNIOR *goes back to listening through the door –*

PRINCESS. Your feet do smell!

LORNA. I like standing.

PRINCESS. What you doing in here? Did you get a slap too? Do you want Junior to give you a lollipop too? It doesn't make the pain go away but it helps.

WENDELL JUNIOR *reaches into his pocket – without looking at* LORNA *pulls out a lollipop – holds it out towards* LORNA –

WENDELL JUNIOR. Here...

LORNA. Daddy says I can't take anything from strangers.

WENDELL JUNIOR. –

PRINCESS. If you don't want it I can /

WENDELL JUNIOR. Princess!

LORNA *snatches the lollipop from* WENDELL JUNIOR*'s hand –*

Beat.

LORNA. I'm Lorna.

PRINCESS. Where did you come from?
    How old are you?
    Do you go to school?
    Why do you speak like that?
    Where's your daddy? /

WENDELL JUNIOR. Stop!

WENDELL JUNIOR *slumps on the bed – lies down and closes his eyes –*

You don't have to know everything. Some things are secret.

PRINCESS. Mrs Turner says it's not good to keep secrets. She says that they are like a bad bellyache. They won't go away until you let it out. She says secrets are the devil's work. Not a good thing ever comes of secrets she says /

WENDELL JUNIOR. You just going to keep on talking?

PRINCESS *throws* WENDELL JUNIOR *a dirty look –*

PRINCESS. I don't have any secrets.
I don't want to have any secrets.
Secrets can eat you up. From the inside like a zombie or a /

WENDELL JUNIOR. You don't know what you're talking about so why don't you just pipe down.

PRINCESS. I do know. I do. Secrets are bad things. They make people do bad things. They make people ugly.
I have never seen anyone with a secret who is beautiful or smiling.

When George wet himself in class and he tried to keep it a secret. Everyone could tell. He is funny-looking so that's not why. He just didn't smile for the whole day. Like his face forgot how to smile and he looked like he was in pain.

Cos that's the thing with secrets sometimes they show anyway.
No need to keep them.
Secret.
No need to keep your mouth all tight like George had to.
No point.
Cos we can see your wet trousers and we can smell it too.

LORNA. Do you ever stop talking?

PRINCESS *moves to the door –*

PRINCESS. Who is that man talking to Mummy Junior?

PRINCESS*'s hand rests on door handle –*

I want to see his face again /

WENDELL JUNIOR. Only if you're after another hard slap on your face.

PRINCESS. You said she wouldn't do it again /

WENDELL JUNIOR. Mummy is…

She wouldn't if it wasn't *him*.

PRINCESS. Why? Why you not being right Junior? I wish
I could start today again! All over again!

Beat.

And Christmas is never going to happen now!

PRINCESS *marches to the bed and throws herself face down
on it* –

WENDELL JUNIOR *sits back down on the bed next to*
PRINCESS –

WENDELL JUNIOR. '*Not even de devil himself going to stop
Christmas inna dis country.*'

PRINCESS *lifts her head from the bed* –
WENDELL JUNIOR *tickles her a little* –
PRINCESS *giggles* –

Beat.

PRINCESS *catches sight of* LORNA *sitting alone. She
jumps up and walks over to where* LORNA *sits* –

PRINCESS (*to* LORNA). You're pretty. And your eyes are
almost blue…

LORNA. They're green.

PRINCESS. I wish my eyes were blue or green or…

Do you want me to show you my dance for the pageant. It's
good isn't it Junior? Want to see…

PRINCESS *doesn't wait for an answer – she takes a place in
front of them and starts her dance routine* –

Scene Five

Half-hour later.

MAVIS, WENDELL JUNIOR *and* PRINCESS *sit tightly together on the small sofa.*

WENDELL *sits in the single armchair with* LORNA *perched next to him.*

Long beat.

MAVIS. This chicken can't cook no more.

Let's eat.

Nobody moves –

Nobody hungry now?

WENDELL. Well one ting hard to forget is yuh cooking Mavis.

WENDELL *moves to the small table –* LORNA *following quickly behind him –*
They sit themselves at the table –

MAVIS *watches* WENDELL JUNIOR –

WENDELL JUNIOR *watches* WENDELL –

PRINCESS *watches* LORNA –

PRINCESS *moves to sit at the table –*

MAVIS. Junior I don't want to tell you again.

PRINCESS. You sit next to me Junior.

Will you?

WENDELL JUNIOR *moves to the table –*
He scrapes the chair noisily away from the table and sits as far away from WENDELL *as possible –*

The chicken is carved up and vegetable distributed in the same way it is being done in homes across the land.

LORNA *picks a fork up –*

WENDELL. No Lorna!

WENDELL puts a hand on LORNA's *arm before the first mouthful goes in –*

MAVIS. We still do this the old-fashioned way.
Our people way.

WENDELL. Yuh wan' me to /

MAVIS. Not your place /

WENDELL. Mi try Mavis /

WENDELL JUNIOR. Feet well and truly under the table.

MAVIS. Hush Junior!

Princess you want to say grace?

LORNA. But Daddy I'm hungry /

PRINCESS. Heavenly Father.
Thank you for this delicious chicken that Mummy has cooked.
Thank you for our Christmas tree that Margot find for us.
Thank you for making Junior not so annoying today.
And thank you...

Beat.

And thank you for giving us more people to feed today.

Beat.

Amen!

A chorus of 'Amens' chime around the table –

MAVIS (*to* LORNA). You can eat now chile!

Long beat.

LORNA *eats ravenously –*

The others eat in silence –

WENDELL. Mavis dis chicken...

WENDELL JUNIOR. Mummy this is the best…

>*Beat.*

LORNA. What's for dessert?

PRINCESS. Eh?

MAVIS. Pardon.

PRINCESS. What?

MAVIS. Phyllis James!

>No *dessert.*

>Apple and spice cake cooling. And I made some custard…

WENDELL. Yuh behave now Lorna.

>(*To* MAVIS.) Juss de way har modder bring har up.

MAVIS. I'm sure.

>'*Manners tek yu thru' di worl'.*'

>Chile…

>Lorna…

LORNA. Yes.

MAVIS. You want any more to eat?

>Plenty of steam vegetable left in the pot.

LORNA. No thank you.

>LORNA *jumps to her feet and leaves the table –*
>*She flops onto the small sofa –*

>PRINCESS *gasps –*

WENDELL. Tanking yuh Mavis.

>MAVIS *kisses her teeth –*

MAVIS. So…

WENDELL. Yes /

MAVIS. Can you let me /

WENDELL. Yes. Sorry /

MAVIS. I want to /

WENDELL. Look how grown you two ar /

MAVIS. Please don't speak.

WENDELL. Of course /

WENDELL JUNIOR. Yes.

WENDELL. Junior.

MAVIS. Hold your tongue.

WENDELL JUNIOR. It's just /

MAVIS. It just what? /

WENDELL. It nuh easy.

MAVIS. You didn't hear me?

WENDELL. Yes.

MAVIS. No. I mean it Wendell.

PRINCESS. Wendell? But Junior your name is Wendell.

MAVIS. Yes Princess /

WENDELL. Princess /

WENDELL JUNIOR. So what?

MAVIS. If you don't let me speak /

WENDELL JUNIOR. Mummy /

PRINCESS. Mummy why you call him Wendell?

MAVIS. Because he is your father!

Beat.

PRINCESS. –

WENDELL. Yes Princess.
    Mi yuh daddy /

WENDELL JUNIOR. Whatever you call it /

MAVIS. Junior!

WENDELL. All of yuhs daddy.

All eyes on LORNA –

PRINCESS *cannot take her eyes off* LORNA –

PRINCESS. My daddy?

MAVIS. Yes.

WENDELL JUNIOR. It takes more than a word to make a father /

MAVIS. Junior!

WENDELL JUNIOR. How long are they staying for?

MAVIS. Princess you done eating?

Or you going to keep chasing them peas round your plate all day and night?

PRINCESS. I can't catch not one of them…

MAVIS *almost laughs watching her daughter* –

PRINCESS *gives up and rests her fork on the plate* –

These peas are too slippery…

MAVIS. Not the only slippery things still here today my dear.

You go and sit with Lorna and…

You want to show her the pictures of beauty queens Margot been giving to you?

PRINCESS. My pictures?

MAVIS. You know everything about them beauty pageants.

Maybe she wants to know too.

PRINCESS. She can never know as much as me. Margot says I have an encyclo… encyclocdo…

I know a lot!

MAVIS. Yes and today you have someone to talk to about them things without bothering me or your brother...

PRINCESS *leaves the table – exits.*

WENDELL JUNIOR. How long are you planning to stay?

MAVIS *puts a finger to her lips to silence him –*

PRINCESS *enters – and sits silently/awkwardly next to* LORNA *on the small sofa –*
She is holding a large folder/book under one arm –

Beat.

The two girls become engrossed in the pictures – whispering excitedly –

The action at the table becomes more focused – speaking in hushed tones/whispers –

MAVIS. Junior you watch your mouth now /

WENDELL JUNIOR. I'm too big to stay quiet /

WENDELL. Yuh big enuff to be ar man dat's far true.

MAVIS. That is no good reason for rudeness.

WENDELL. Mi understand how de bwoy feeling still.

MAVIS *walks towards the girls on the sofa –*

MAVIS. Why don't you two girls take them photos and lay them down on my bed. See them better that way.

PRINCESS *and* LORNA *exit – still engrossed in the book of photos –*

You sit here for all of ten minutes, and now you feel you can tell me about my own children?

WENDELL. Juss sayin' Mavis.
Mi ar growing bwoy once.

Dese tings take ar lickle understanding.

Particula' overstanding.

MAVIS (*turning to* WENDELL JUNIOR). We're giving them food for today.

All my Christian duty can stretch to.

WENDELL. We 'ave no place to go Mavis /

MAVIS. I can make a bed up for the little one…

WENDELL JUNIOR. Can I leave the table?

MAVIS. I can't turn away the child…

WENDELL JUNIOR *exits*.

WENDELL *and* MAVIS *stare each other down* –

Long beat.

WENDELL. It really very kind of yuh to take mercy on us. Yuh know only so much ar man kyaan do when it come to looking after children dem.

You will be rewarded in heaven Mavis.

You nuh hear me breathe till wi get to sekkle somewhere /

MAVIS. No!

I did not say *you* could stay Wendell.
And you do good to remember I am only doing this for that little one.
If not for pity for the child, I would happily cut out your dirty tongue from your mouth!

WENDELL. Mi kyannt wander street. Where mi gon stay?

MAVIS. Wendell. I don't care.

You come get the child when you find somewhere. And if you don't come back in a matter of days, then I hand her over to Salvation Army themselves /

WENDELL. What 'appen far yuh to get so cruel Mavis? De Mavis I remember never tark like dis. De woman mi 'ave dem children wit /

MAVIS. Wha' ya say? De Mavis you wha?…

MAVIS *stands up and slaps* WENDELL *across the face –*

De Mavis you leff you mean? She dead!

WENDELL *jumps to his feet – backing off all the time –
whilst* MAVIS *walks towards him – pushing him –*

An' today dis cold-heart woman… she born de day mi wake
and find my husband gone!

Mi nearly starve my children waiting 'pon you. Walking
street fram Southmead to Hotwells looking far yuh.

MAVIS *points in the direction where her heart should be –*

Nothing here for *yuh*! An' only nuff far the bastard child you
choose to have!

WENDELL *grabs his jacket –*

De girl will be here waiting for you tomorrow.

WENDELL *opens the front door –*

MARGOT *enters/bursts in.*

WENDELL *jumps back –*

MARGOT. Someone say my name?!

MAVIS. Margot!

What are you doing here?

MARGOT. Not much.

Just passing in the corridor.

And heard voices…

Voices like I never heard before…

MARGOT *stares directly at* WENDELL –

And you know I'm not one to poke it where it's not wanted
but…
Well it looks like I was right.

Voices…

MARGOT *glides over to* WENDELL –
Her voice like butter-wouldn't-melt –

Faces I never heard or seen before.

MAVIS. You're back? /

MARGOT. My name is Margot Barker.

Named after Margot Fonteyn /

MARGOT *holds a hand out to* WENDELL –

WENDELL *nods politely and puts his coat down on the chair –*

WENDELL. Good to meet you.

MAVIS. Thought you still away for next two days at least /

MARGOT. So did I Mavis!
So did I.

MARGOT *pulls up a chair very close to* WENDELL *and takes a seat –*
Crossing her legs seductively –

But turns out my sister-in-law's nothing more than one of the witches from that play…

What 'em call it? The one by Shakespeare…

MAVIS. *Macbeth*?

MARGOT. Yeah that's the one.

MAVIS. You can't talk like that about family.

MARGOT. If you had the displeasure of her face you would have a few choice words too.

Had barely got through the pleasantries before she started on her high-and-mighty speeches about them living with less. The *damned poor* as she likes to call 'em.

Calling each and every one something mean. Scums she would say in between mouthfuls of porridge. Horrible and mean. And well I'm choking on my cuppa. Right mare!

And as we all know I'm living here purely by choice, and well the working-class blood don't quite run through these veins, and I'm no socialist, but couldn't sit there and listen to 'nuffer minute of it.

MAVIS. You walked out?

MARGOT. Well I would of walked out.

If only the silly cow dinned start throwing all my stuff out the door first. Dinned have much choice. Asking me to keep my filthy language to myself. Well she hadn't even heard all I had to say before she threw my best.

You know that fur I'm always promising little Princess? Nearly lost that in the scrap.

Where is my Princess?
Missed that little chicken.

And what's for Christmas dinner then?

MAVIS. We've eaten Margot.

MARGOT. Will have to be a sherry and a mince pie then /

MAVIS. No mince pies /

MARGOT. Well many a sailor have done good with sherry alone /

MAVIS. We are a little busy.

MARGOT. Right.

Nowhere else to go and spending Christmas alone it is for me then.

WENDELL. Mi an' yuh both /

MAVIS. We are just *discussing* a few things...

Be no fun for you to be hanging around /

MARGOT. Don't mind me!

MARGOT *throws herself on the armchair –*

Anything going on in these four walls none of my business mind.

WENDELL. Mi nuh say no to ar lickle something hot mi self /

MAVIS. I have no sherry!

MARGOT. Not like you Mavis. Always have everything a guest
could ask for in your cupboards.

WENDELL. She de kindest woman mi know. If yuh like it so
mi kyaan go buy something. Be good to sit ar lickle an' meet
some of dem good people inna yuh life.

MARGOT *gestures a prayer to* MAVIS –

MAVIS. If it keep you quiet!

WENDELL *slaps/rubs his hands together* –

WENDELL. Mi an' de bwoy kyaan go to ar liquor store.

MARGOT. Offie?

WENDELL. Yes dat's de one. Buy dis woman a drink.

Be good to take ar walk. Get to know how de land lie ar lickle.

MARGOT. I can get this one…

MARGOT *reaches into her handbag and pulls out some
notes* –

MAVIS. No!
There is no drink in the house because I was not expecting
any guests. If any guest turn up on their own accord, then
they should bring a bottle as a matter of *respect*.

MARGOT *stifles a laugh* –
Beat.

WENDELL. Maybe mi kyaan find ar lickle someting in dis old
coat pocket…

WENDELL *walks towards his coat* –
Puts it on –
Searches pockets briefly –

WENDELL *cocks his head at* MAVIS *and* MARGOT –

WENDELL *exits.*

MAVIS (*shouting after* WENDELL). Only when he has
something to run from!

MAVIS *busies herself clearing the table* –

MARGOT *watches* MAVIS *intently* –

MARGOT. Well…

Christmas a day for joy and good tidings…
And we just the picture of 'em Christmas cards sat here.

Nice tree. …

MAVIS *pulls out a bottle of rum from a cupboard* –
Holds it out to MARGOT –

Mavis James!

MARGOT *helps herself to a glass on the table and quickly
pours a drink* –

Beat.

Saw Mrs Bowen day before. She was chirping away at your
handiwork for all to hear in the grocer's mind. Said you gone
and made better curtains than 'em in Marks and Sparks.
Every pleat exactly where it should be.

MAVIS. She's always very good to me.

MARGOT. Well she would be!

MAVIS. Why?

MARGOT. Well you're one and the same so be a bit odd to be
against your own /

MAVIS. Not this again!

MAVIS *stops clearing – holds her head in her hands* –

Beat.

MARGOT. You feeling okay Mavis?

Things seem very strange in 'ere.

And your face reminding me of someone who might have just seen a ghost in the flesh...

Dinned know you had a brother. Seems nice /

MAVIS. He is not my brother.
Can't you see?

MARGOT. Barely know my nose is there most days.
You're going to have to give me a bit more /

MAVIS. Even after all these years, and that ridiculous moustache...
Him still the same man.
Nothing changed on his face.

MAVIS *traces the contours of her face –*

And me...

MARGOT. Wait!
You mean...

MAVIS. Yes.

MARGOT. No!!

I mean he is a good-looking fella.
But I'm with you,
Moustache a bit off if you asks me.

PRINCESS *enters –*

PRINCESS. Margot!

PRINCESS *runs towards* MARGOT *and wraps her arms around her as high as she can reach –*

MARGOT. Princess!

PRINCESS. You got any more pictures Margot?

LORNA *enters –*

MARGOT. Who's your friend Princess?

PRINCESS. She's not my friend. She's my sister /

MAVIS. Princess! /

MARGOT. Your what?

> Ark at ee!
> A sister eh?
> Bets that's the best Christmas present you ever had.
>
> Hello.
> My name is Margot.

PRINCESS. Her name is Lorna.

MARGOT. Hi Lorna.

> (*To* MAVIS.) I mean look at that!
> She must be half half /

MAVIS. Ssshhh…

PRINCESS. Margot can we come to your room and look
    through your dresses?
    And you can tell Lorna all about Weston. And the beach and
    the donkeys and /

MAVIS. Not today Princess /

MARGOT. Got nothing better to be doing with my time, and
    I reckons you could do with having a bit of time to yourself…

> Maybe tidy yourself up a little?

MAVIS. You spoil her.

MARGOT. We'll be just down the corridor if you need us.
    Stop worrying.
    Put on a nice dress.
    You look lush when you give yourself a bit of time in
    the mirror.

> MARGOT *pushes her cleavage up –*

> Need a whole half-hour just to get these puppies looking
> right most mornings.

MAVIS. Margot!

MARGOT. That's more like it. The Mavis I know and love.

Come on mi babbers. Let's be having some dressing up!

MARGOT *exits – quickly followed by* PRINCESS *and*
LORNA.

MAVIS *moves to stand at a mirror –*
She looks closely at the lines on her face –

MAVIS *exits into the bedroom.*

Scene Six

Three days later.

PRINCESS *and* LORNA *sit on a couple of crates – looking*
extremely bored.

PRINCESS. Daddy!

Daddy!

LORNA. I'm hungry.

PRINCESS. I'm tired.

LORNA. We've been waiting for ages.

PRINCESS. You said we were going to the park…

LORNA. It's been a long time now…

PRINCESS. You said we could feed the birds…

LORNA. And have chocolate.

PRINCESS. We haven't had chocolate…

LORNA. Or been to the park.

PRINCESS. We haven't done anything actually…

LORNA. For a long time now…

PRINCESS. Just been sitting here…

LORNA. Waiting…

PRINCESS. And waiting…

LORNA. And I want to go home now…

PRINCESS. And I'm going to tell Mummy!

> WENDELL *enters full of cheer – a bundle of money in his hands. He stands with his back to* PRINCESS *and* LORNA. *He carefully folds the bundle, and puts it into his pocket – leaving a single note out.*

WENDELL. Yuh girls nuh appreciate ar single ting. Yuh know where unu stay?

PRINCESS. We are at the docks. There's nothing special here and it smells.

WENDELL. Of steel an' de sweat of hard-workin' men.

LORNA. They don't look like they're sweating.

WENDELL. Dem shipbuilding. Hard work. Good hard-workin' people.

PRINCESS. They don't seem to be working that hard. They're sitting around playing cards with you.

WENDELL. Everybody need ar break!

> WENDELL *whips his fingers together – in victorious mood. He waves the single note in front of the girls.*

So now mi going take mi darters out far ar lickle chocolate an' ting. Then maybe buy my Princess – es – some toys. Unno wan' far nothing yuh hear!

PRINCESS. Can we go now?

WENDELL. Mi juss 'ave to tark to one man dere…

> Yuh girls stay right 'ere. You nuh move fram 'ere! I juss need to tark to one man 'bout ar dog.

> WENDELL *exits.*

In unison –

PRINCESS *and* LORNA. Puppies!!

Beat.

PRINCESS. What was Liverpool like?
Is it the same?
Or is it different?
It must be different because you speak different. Have you
been speaking different since you were a baby Lorna?
I like how you speak…

LORNA. –

PRINCESS *leans in –*

PRINCESS. Do you like living in Bristol?

Beat.

Bristol is nice and all but really I think we should move and
live in Weston-super-Mare.

Would you like to live in Weston-super-Mare Lorna?

LORNA. I don't know it. I only know home.

PRINCESS. Don't worry when we go to the pageant with
Margot, we will see Weston. You will see it really is magic.
It has a beach and sand. Golden sand. And they don't have
just ice cream, Margot says they have *choc ices*. And
donkeys. And everyone there is beautiful that is why they
have the pageant there. But don't worry Lorna we won't talk
to any boys. Boys get you into trouble Mummy says. Did
your mummy ever say that?

LORNA. No. She never really said anything like that.

PRINCESS. Where is your mummy Lorna?

LORNA. Having a rest Daddy said.

PRINCESS. Everyone needs a rest…

Beat.

LORNA. Princess do you want me to stay here forever?

PRINCESS. If you stay here forever I will be happier than the sky Lorna.

But I understand if you have to go away. I missed my daddy even though I couldn't remember him. If you miss your mummy too much, then I will understand. But I will be sad...

Will you be sad Lorna?

WENDELL JUNIOR *and* LEON *enter – cameras in hand.*

PRINCESS *and* LORNA *run towards him. He hugs them tightly.*

Junior!

LEON. Is this...?

WENDELL JUNIOR. Yeah.

LEON. You didn't say she...

WENDELL JUNIOR. Lorna this is my good friend Leon.

Say hello.

LORNA. –

LEON. Hello Lorna.

PRINCESS. Hi Leon!

LEON. Is this a real-life Princess talking to me?

PRINCESS. Yes.

LEON *bows – picks* PRINCESS *up and spins her around – puts her down again –*

WENDELL JUNIOR. Why you here?

Princess answer me!

PRINCESS. We're... we're...

LORNA. Waiting for my daddy /

PRINCESS. Our daddy!

WENDELL JUNIOR. He brought you here? Where is he now?

Why are you waiting for him all alone like this?

PRINCESS. He said he needed to talk to a man about a dog.

LORNA. We're getting a puppy!

LEON (*to* WENDELL JUNIOR). Your mum won't like that!

WENDELL JUNIOR. Right.

WENDELL JUNIOR *grunts with frustration – takes a deep breath –*

Think you two should go back and tell Mummy all about it.

PRINCESS. Daddy said we are not to move.

LEON. This is no place for young girls. There is grown men and dirt and machinery.

WENDELL JUNIOR. Leon can you take them home for me. I'll wait for him to come back.

LEON *tries to grab hold of the girls' hands. They struggle with him.*

LEON. Guess you don't want to pass by the sweet shop on the way back then?

PRINCESS *and* LORNA *stop their fuss – and obediently hook their arms together and follow* LEON *– exiting.*

WENDELL JUNIOR *takes a seat on one of the crates – and waits!*

WENDELL JUNIOR *takes pictures as he waits.*

Time passes at the docks.

WENDELL *enters.*

WENDELL. Junior!

WENDELL *goes to pat* WENDELL JUNIOR *on the back –* WENDELL JUNIOR *flinches and moves away –*

Where yuh sisters?

WENDELL JUNIOR. They went home.

WENDELL. Yuh leff dem to walk all de way back on dem own?

WENDELL JUNIOR. No. But you left them here waiting in this place on their own.

WENDELL. Mi juss leave dem far ar minute. Mi nuh gone long.

Yuh did ar good thing sending dem home anyways /

WENDELL JUNIOR. Don't bring them here again. The docks is not a place for them.

WENDELL. Okay. Okay. Mi hear yuh loud an' correct.

Where you passing through fram? De way you boys move round de city dese days...

WENDELL *produced a pack of cards from his pocket –*

Yuh wan' run ar game of cards?

WENDELL JUNIOR. No.

WENDELL. What 'bout ar run of Cut-Throat?

Yuh looking at de champion of champions.

Beat.

WENDELL JUNIOR. Only thing I want is for you to go!

WENDELL. Wah?!

WENDELL JUNIOR. You heard me. You want to be down here playing cards then go ahead but keep us out of it.

We're doing fine without you.

WENDELL. Son...

WENDELL *reaches out and grabs* WENDELL JUNIOR*'s arm –*

WENDELL JUNIOR *jerks away from* WENDELL*'s grasp – stands up –*

Mi come to make good son. Make right /

WENDELL JUNIOR. Make trouble more like.

WENDELL. Why yuh say dat? Dat wha' yuh modder tell yuh?

WENDELL JUNIOR *turns his back to* WENDELL –

Beat.

Mi know mi do wrong in de past. Yuh 'ave ebbry right to be angry.

Mi spirit troubled since de day mi leff yuh an' yuh modder but ebbryone deserve ar second chance. Yuh nuh say so?

WENDELL JUNIOR *turns to face* WENDELL –

WENDELL JUNIOR. You're a liar! Everyone knows it.

WENDELL. Dis stink-up attitude 'ave to end some time mi son. Some time cus only so long mi put up wit dis kinda disrespect yuh know.

WENDELL JUNIOR. So? So what you going to do about it?

WENDELL. Mi nuh business wit yuh son /

WENDELL JUNIOR. Yeah I know. You're not here for me. Or for Princess or even for Lorna. You've come back just so you can leave again. That's what you want isn't it? To break us all over again.

I won't let you…

Quicker than imaginable, WENDELL JUNIOR *grabs* WENDELL *by the neck, they struggle with each other until* WENDELL *has* WENDELL JUNIOR *pinned up against the wall –*

WENDELL JUNIOR *doesn't resist –*

WENDELL. Inna yuh shoes mi too be ready to break ar man but yuh kyannt put yuh hand 'pon yuh fadder Junior. Yuh kyannt do it nuh matter what pain yuh.

WENDELL *lets go of* WENDELL JUNIOR *and straightens himself up –*

Mi juss wan' talk to you son. Mi know mi 'ave ar long way to go before yuh look 'pon mi like ar fadder again. An' wha mi do to yuh modder…

Mi proud of yuh far protectin' yuh modder an' sister but yuh 'ave to tell mi wha' mi do 'bout dis business.

Mi here to do what mi kyann to be ar good fadder and ar 'usband. Nuthing yuh kyaan do to change dat. So yuh need to fix up yuh attitude Junior. Cus yuh see son, no matter how yuh carry on, De Hustler back!

WENDELL *fixes the hat on his head and moves to leave –*

An' when mi start making big big money yuh soon be telling everybody in dis Bristol who yuh daddy be. Yuh be proud son. Mi nuh leave till mi make yuh proud as ar peacock. Yuh hear mi?

WENDELL JUNIOR *slumps back down on the crate – and cries hard hot tears –*

Scene Seven

St Agnes, Bristol. January 1963.

PRINCESS, LORNA *and* MARGOT *sit at the table – the girls busy drawing –* MARGOT *is reading a magazine.*

WENDELL *enters.*
He is wrapped in blankets and shivering a little.

PRINCESS *and* LORNA. Daddy!

    Both girls run to throw their arms around WENDELL –

MARGOT. Oh!

    I wasn't expecting any visitors…

WENDELL. Mi juss come far ar lickle something hot /

MARGOT. There's a caff down the road /

WENDELL. Mi 'ave juss pennies in mi pocket /

MARGOT. That right?

WENDELL. Mi 'ave every right to come see mi children an'
mi wife /

MARGOT. She's not here mind so…

WENDELL *sits –*

WENDELL. Mi wait…

MARGOT. If you want!

PRINCESS. You're cold Daddy.

WENDELL. Yes mi know Princess. Still sleeping where mi
kyaan find.

Juss need ar lickle coffee fi warm up my flesh an' bones /

MARGOT. Alright mi babbers you go in your room now and
clean up that mess we made earlier cos I don't want to be
here if your mother sees it like that.

WENDELL. Bible or belt.

WENDELL *laughs at his own joke –*

PRINCESS *and* LORNA *exit.*

MARGOT. Yes but she got a lot of heart too. Looks after
everyone. And I look after her.

WENDELL. Dat very good of *yuh.*

MARGOT. You ask anyone on this street, they'll tell you Mavis
and me are always together. I help her out and she…

She looks out for me. And not one of *'em* messes with me
because they know I'm with Mavis. That's how it works
round 'ere.

That's what you do for family. You look after *your* family.
You go out. You get a decent job /

WENDELL. Fram where?
I take mi self down to dat job exchange every day. Standing in
dat line far hours in dat smelly, smoky, crowded office room.
An' after mi come out of dere, walk de whole ar de street
knocking on shop daw an' factory askin' far any employment.

Still nutting!
If rumours true den dem nuh wan' us far any work!

MARGOT. Well it has been a long time since you been here...

Things changing. They've changed in here. And they're changing out there too.

WENDELL JUNIOR enters with LEON *in tow –*
WENDELL JUNIOR stares at WENDELL *–*
He walks silently to chair, sits and plays with his camera –
LEON *stays standing awkwardly –*

Junior? You alright handsome?

WENDELL JUNIOR. What's he doing here?

LEON. Hello Mrs...

Margot...

MARGOT. Leon you growing into a real man too I see. Guess you two have the young girls all after you.

LEON. No time for girls. Want a real woman.

LEON *moves closer to* MARGOT *–*

MARGOT *moves closer to* LEON *–*

I'm working now. Got income. Enough to take a woman out dancing /

MARGOT. And which woman you think you're going to be dancing with chicken?

LEON. Well...

LEON *attempts to casually lean on a wall and slips –*

MARGOT *moves back to* WENDELL JUNIOR *–*

MARGOT. Junior you not yourself these days.

WENDELL JUNIOR. Things not so right *here* any more.

LEON. Things are looking good from where I'm standing!

MARGOT *throws* LEON *an exasperated look –*

WENDELL. Yuh 'ave nowhere you 'ave to be Margot now Junior 'ere?

MARGOT. I do actually!

MARGOT *walks over to* WENDELL JUNIOR –

You alright to keep an eye out for your sisters? I have to go help out with that am-dram lot again for an hour or so. Don't know why I signed up now. When a charitable deed must be done, well it seems I always ends up being called in. It's like people can see all that kindness and goodness pouring out of me. When you've got a face like this, you have to be careful people don't take advantage...

Even though I wouldn't mind the caretaker taking advantage once in a while /

WENDELL. Watch yuh words, dem juss boys.

LEON *coughs* –

WENDELL JUNIOR. I'm not a boy! You think I don't know about the world. About what it means to be a man... a Black man /

MARGOT. Anyways *Junior* make sure your ma don't get upset about nothing when she gets back in.

MARGOT *squeezes* WENDELL JUNIOR*'s cheeks* –
She smiles a dry smile at WENDELL –
She saunters past LEON *and exits.*

Long beat.

WENDELL. Junior...

WENDELL JUNIOR. –

WENDELL. Junior. Mi come to talk far true.

LEON (*whispering*). Look I better be going...

LEON *stands* –

WENDELL JUNIOR. You said you show me that thing with the aperture again /

WENDELL. You hear mi?

LEON. It's just /

WENDELL JUNIOR. Leon you said!

LEON. Told my dad I've go help him set up for this meeting thing.

WENDELL JUNIOR. At the boys' club?

LEON. You know what his 'disappointed in you' face is like.

WENDELL JUNIOR. Yes.

LEON. Sorry.

WENDELL JUNIOR. Think there's still talk about a colour bar /

WENDELL. De rumours true den? About dem stopping upright men fram working?

LEON. Likely.

WENDELL JUNIOR. Wish I was coming with /

WENDELL. Mi nuh see you far ar few days…

WENDELL JUNIOR. It's just… I can't… leave my sisters /

WENDELL. If yuh wan' step out, mi stay wit dem girls /

WENDELL JUNIOR. I wouldn't trust you with a dog!

LEON. Junior!

WENDELL. Yuh wan' fight mi every time bwoy?

WENDELL JUNIOR *jumps to his feet –*

WENDELL JUNIOR. Why not!

WENDELL *moves towards* WENDELL JUNIOR –

WENDELL. Just trying to be a father /

WENDELL JUNIOR. Don't need you! Leon's daddy looks out for me fine. Lent me this camera. Said I could have it as Mummy dinned have enough… And gave me the paper round in his shop so I could save up. A man should have saving he said. Dinned he Leon?

Leon's daddy been more of a daddy to me than you!

WENDELL. Dat so!

WENDELL JUNIOR. He's a good man. Does for other people not just himself.

WENDELL. Is it? You wan' hear some good things mi do too. Mi used to cut a man's hair good back in de day.

Beat.

What 'im do so impressive?

WENDELL JUNIOR. Getting involved in the protests. Standing up for good things.

WENDELL. Protest? Here in Bristol?

Dis true Leon?

WENDELL JUNIOR *stares hard at* WENDELL –

LEON. Yes. If people start making noise, they will take notice. That's what my dad says anyway.

WENDELL. Dat true!

If yuh daddy involve maybe mi kyaan /

WENDELL JUNIOR *laughs hard and loud –*

WENDELL JUNIOR. I already warn Leon not to believe anything you say!

WENDELL *kisses his teeth and moves to pour himself another drink –*

LEON. I have to go.

WENDELL JUNIOR *stands –*
He shakes his head at LEON *to try to make him stay –*

LEON *grabs* WENDELL JUNIOR *by the shoulders and pulls him towards the front door – out of* WENDELL's *earshot –*

Cool it Junior.

You dig?

WENDELL JUNIOR. It's just /

LEON. He's your daddy. He deserves a little…

Stay cool.

Yeah?

WENDELL JUNIOR. Yes yes!

You think my photos are getting better Leon?

LEON. Maybe!

WENDELL JUNIOR *and* LEON *laugh – and touch hands –*

LEON *exits.*

WENDELL JUNIOR *moves to go to his room –*

WENDELL. Come talk to me /

WENDELL JUNIOR. I need to read.

WENDELL *reaches to grab* WENDELL JUNIOR –

WENDELL JUNIOR *shrugs him off –*

WENDELL. Junior yuh gon' 'ave tark to me man to man some time?
Mi need to explain some tings to *yuh* /

WENDELL JUNIOR. You know what they call a boy without a father round here?
Do you?
Bastard!
A bloody bastard! /

WENDELL. Mi beg yuh stop!

When mi come to dis country I was ar good man.
Ar soldier.
Fight far King an' country.
But it never make far respec'.

Fram dis Englishman.

Dem just throw mi out of the army, and expect mi to live on air.

Mi try to make it work for all af us.

Truly.

But here…

Beat.

Even now everywhere mi go looking far work, dem look at mi so so…

An' grown men wit ar family scratching around far even ar paper round.

Wha' kinda world?!

Wha' kinda world put men in de same sentence as dogs?

Supm 'ave ta change fram de days of mi ancestors.

'Ave ta!

WENDELL *pours himself a large drink –*

WENDELL JUNIOR. Why have you come back? It still the same. Nothing is different /

WENDELL. Mi trying to tark to yuh straight…

WENDELL JUNIOR. Sounds like excuses to me.

WENDELL. Excuses?

WENDELL JUNIOR. Lots of excuses.

WENDELL JUNIOR *gets up to leave –*

WENDELL. Yuh nuh live yet.

Yuh young'un still.

One day yuh understand.

Lorna's modder…

She kind.

Give mi time an' ar roof over mi head when de squat got raided.

Wi juss living together for ar while.

No-ting more.

But den…

Well wit de right music an' drink…

An' ar lickle moonlight…
Tings 'appen.
Den odder tings 'appen nine months later.
An' I could've leff it at dat.
Yes I could've gone den an' dere.
But mi remember unu.
'Pon mi modder's life mi never forget yuh.
Yuh an' ya sister an'…
Tink only ar fool make ar mistake like dat twice.
Leave anodder chile?
Nuh mi kyannt do it.
Mi juss kyannt do it.
And ting is…
Lorna modder not well.
In de head.
Yuh understand?
She start show signs.
Har heart good, but har mind trouble beyon' help.
After she done screaming de street down 'bout de black devil
who come an' possess her.
Rape har.
So dey take har arway one day.
'Ave to hold har firm all de way to de hospital.

People start writing all sort of nonsense 'pon mi door.
On de house.
Windows break every day till one day mi come back to find
ar rope hanging fram de tree outside de house.
An' I never plan to be nuh strange fruit.
Yuh understand son.
Never plan dat.

WENDELL JUNIOR. Well at least you didn't leave in the
middle of the night this time.

Beat.

WENDELL. I leave in de mawnin'. Juss as yuh waking /

WENDELL JUNIOR. I didn't know the difference between
early morning and night.

I didn't know the difference between another day and
goodbye.
(*Shouting*.) Why are you even talking to me about these
things /

MAVIS enters.

MAVIS. Junior! You want to get us the reputation of being like
them angry Black people?

WENDELL. It not 'im fault Mavis. Wi juss 'aving ar lickle man
till man.

Beat.

Why yuh always 'ave to be de prettiest gyal 'pon de street?

MAVIS kisses her teeth loudly –

MAVIS. The girls eat yet? Princess! Lorna!

PRINCESS and LORNA run out of the other room –

WENDELL JUNIOR exits.

PRINCESS. Mummy! It's the best thing in the world having
a sister. We were holding hands all through the market, and
everyone wants to talk to us.
Everyone was saying we must be sisters because I tell them
everything Lorna likes and /

MAVIS. Princess James you going to let Lorna speak for herself?
Lorna you like the market?

WENDELL. Sound like de girls 'ave a busy day /

MAVIS. We can't all be idle.

You come to collect her then?

LORNA. Are we going home Daddy?

WENDELL. No.
Mavis. Mi looking everywhere far some place decent to put
mi head down but only manage to find ar few old friends
who 'ave ar chair or two. Mi kyannt be moving ar young girl
dis way an' dat /

MAVIS. Well it take as long as it take. She safe and happy
here until…
You like it here Lorna?

Beat.

WENDELL. Answer when yuh been asked ar question Lorna.

LORNA. Yes Daddy. I like having a sister.

WENDELL. I juss come to warm up an' check on mi girls…

I better be going…

WENDELL *gets to his feet – feebly and unsteady –*

PRINCESS. Mummy!

MAVIS. Yes Princess.

PRINCESS. If someone is cold all the time, you wouldn't let
them stay out in the cold would you? You're too kind like
that aren't you Mummy?

And you always say that '*God watch the devil in people all
the time.*'

WENDELL *stifles a laugh –*

Daddy could share a room with Junior.

And then we would all be together, and Lorna wouldn't cry
at night so much…

MAVIS. Why didn't you tell me she been crying?

Long beat.

WENDELL. Yuh nuh worry Mavis. Yuh already done good by
us dese last few weeks…

MAVIS. Go tell Junior to make up the beds while I cook. You
girls will have to come in with me.

PRINCESS. We can help Junior make the beds. I'm good at
making beds.

PRINCESS *hooks her arm into* LORNA*'s – they exeunt.*

MAVIS. The rules simple.
    You sleep only in that room.
    You never walk around the house half-dressed /

WENDELL. Mi know de temptation dat come over woman
    when mi inna small vest.

    MAVIS *gives him the coldest stare imaginable –*

MAVIS. You use the bathroom only after we all done getting
    ready for school and work. You wash every plate and spoon
    you use.
    You never bring no woman into this house. You never bring
    no friend into this house. And you have just two weeks to
    find somewhere else to take yourself and that child.

WENDELL. Mavis mi kyannt tank yuh enuff. All mi want is to
    be here with mi family /

MAVIS. You listen to mi good Wendell. If you so much as look
    or do mi or mi children de wrong way, mi call de police on
    you. An' mi personally tell dem to lock you up far good. Still
    things I remember that can put you an' your backside inna
    police cell. You remember dat!

    MAVIS *exits.*

    WENDELL *sits back down at the table and smiles wryly
    to himself –*

ACT TWO

Scene One

St Agnes, Bristol. May 1963.

MAVIS *sits at the table.*
Her sewing machine tapping rhythmically.

PRINCESS *and* LORNA *enter.*

PRINCESS *is dressed in school uniform.*

PRINCESS *has her head down.*
She runs to the sofa and throws herself across it sobbing loudly.

LORNA *stands holding a school bag.*

MAVIS. What happen *today*?
  That teacher saying meanness to you again?
  Those teachers need to realise they can't keep putting my
  children on some dunce table.

  Tomorrow I'm going /

Another loud sob from PRINCESS –

Beat.

  Phyllis James are you not going to answer me?

Beat.

LORNA. She was crying hard all the way home.

MAVIS. Why?

  WENDELL *enters.*
  He is holding a big box –

LORNA. Daddy!!

  LORNA *runs to* WENDELL –

Hugging him –

WENDELL *puts the box down –*

MAVIS *doesn't take her eyes off the box –*

WENDELL. Hello Princess…

I mean…

All mi favourite girls inna one room.

LORNA. Daddy when are we going home?

WENDELL. I tell yuh already 'bout asking dat.

MAVIS. What you bringing in my house Wendell James?

WENDELL. Just a little something I pick up fram ar man…

For Junior!

MAVIS *gestures at* WENDELL –

An' how is my Princess today?

Beat.

WENDELL *stands over* PRINCESS *who is still motionless –*

How school go Princess?

WENDELL *kneels down –*
He taps PRINCESS *gently –*

Baby girl?

Yuh know mi go by dat shop with all dem princesses dress today. De real pretty ones /

LORNA. I know why she is crying.

MAVIS. Someone saying mean things on the way home?

LORNA. No.

MAVIS. She fall and hurt herself?

LORNA. No.

MAVIS. –

LORNA. I think it was…

> She wasn't crying before. But then she started to cry.
> Or maybe she was crying before but I only hear it after /

WENDELL. After what Lorna?

LORNA. After Barbara invited me to her birthday party.

> Says there's going to be a big cake and a clown.

> A real-life clown!

MAVIS. Why would that make her cry?
That girl love cake like people love Jesus!

LORNA. She didn't invite Phyllis.

MAVIS. She invite only you?

LORNA. Yes…

WENDELL. Children!

> PRINCESS *jumps up suddenly and exits to the bedroom* –

LORNA. And she started crying. Crying all the way home…

> I want to go to Barbara's party Daddy. Barbara says that
> I can even wear my hair like hers if I like /

WENDELL. Did *she*?

MAVIS. No one going to no birthday party with such a mean girl /

LORNA. But she asked *me*.

> Daddy I can go can't I?

WENDELL. It nuh dat simple Lorna.

> Yuh sister /

LORNA. But Barbara says she can't invite Phyllis!

MAVIS. And why is that?

WENDELL. Mavis!

> Lissen Lorna. Dere is nuh talking on dis. If yuh sister nuh
> good nuff far har party den yuh not good nuff far har party.
> Dat simple.

LORNA *stomps off in a huff – exits.*

Beat.

MAVIS. You don't think to educate that girl?

She is going to learn the hard way one day.

WENDELL. Where she come fram dese things nuh spoken
'bout Mavis /

MAVIS. But she half come from you so /

WENDELL. Why yuh always on mi?

MAVIS. Maybe because I have more than enough experience of
you not doing what you're suppose to do for your family.

WENDELL. Yuh nuh see mi trying?

WENDELL *starts to undo his shoes –*

MAVIS. Once a hustler always a hustler!

WENDELL. Mi show yuh Mavis!

Yuh juss 'ave ta give mi ar lickle chance.

Ar lickle chance to be ar better man.

MAVIS. For what? So you can go running back to Liverpool?

WENDELL. Lissen 'ere. Dat business over. Over.

MAVIS. I don't care to hear about it.

Beat.

WENDELL. Yuh de woman far me.

Remember how it used to be?
Remember how wi used to laugh. Like children ourselves.
Yuh sitting on mi knee.
Drinking rum.
Yuh face all bright…
Still is…
Yuh lips always juss de right shade of pretty.
An' yuh legs Mavis…
Still…

MAVIS. Right now you're talking like a madman.

WENDELL. Mi juss saying yuh legs enuff to drive ar wild man
    'alf outta 'im mind /

MAVIS. You want to talk about my legs?
    What about these hands that been doing the work of two
    people? /

WENDELL. Mavis /

MAVIS. Wendell how you think we have food? When mi nuh
    here sewing till my fingers turn blue, mi out there asking
    every woman if she need a new dress. Then I come back and
    sew them ones too!

    MAVIS *is close to tears* −

WENDELL. One day dem hands nuh work no more mi promise.

    It only ar matter of time before I find mi ar lickle pay packet.
    Den mi buy ar house − ar 'hol' house far mi wife. Ar house
    wit ar staircase, ar garden, inna better street. Nuh dis place
    where everybody live on top of everybody.

    WENDELL *stands, walks towards* MAVIS *and pulls her to
    a small window* −

    Yuh look out de winda Mavis. What yuh see? Juss de backa
    more house. Nuh trees. Nuh hills like back home. Yuh nuh
    worry.
    Only ar matter of time before mi start to give yuh de best in
    life an' take yuh out ageen. No worries mi whine yuh off
    dem feet…

    WENDELL *in one quick movement grabs* MAVIS *and spins
    her fast in a dance* −

MAVIS. Wendell!
    You lost your mind?

    They spin faster −

    You nothing more than a jack − ass!

    MAVIS *laughs out loud* −

WENDELL. Like dem first dances in ar Monty's.
Remember?

MAVIS. I remember.

WENDELL. An' den slow dance when mi pull yuh up close…

WENDELL *pulls* MAVIS *close by the waist –*

An' wi push up 'pon each other till de last person leave /

MAVIS. –

WENDELL JUNIOR *enters.*

MAVIS *jumps out of* WENDELL*'s embrace –*

WENDELL. Son /

MAVIS. Where you been Junior?

WENDELL. I find something far yuh /

WENDELL JUNIOR. I'm going to my room /

WENDELL. If yuh juss give mi ar minute of yuh time…

WENDELL JUNIOR *moves towards the other room –*

WENDELL *moves to pick up the box –*

No wait! Junior! It ar piece of equipment…

He hands it to WENDELL JUNIOR *–*

WENDELL JUNIOR *tentatively opens it –*

WENDELL JUNIOR. Oh!

WENDELL. You like it son?

MAVIS. What is it? Junior? It junk?

WENDELL *kisses his teeth –*

WENDELL JUNIOR. No.
It's a Tully flash.

MAVIS. What?

WENDELL JUNIOR. A light. I've been reading about it and
now…

MAVIS. Well education is never a bad thing.

WENDELL JUNIOR *goes towards his room* –

Junior you forget your mind. I haven't heard thank you yet.

WENDELL JUNIOR *turns to face* WENDELL –

WENDELL JUNIOR. Thank you.

WENDELL. How yuh paying far dose books den Junior?

WENDELL JUNIOR. Got more hours at the shop delivering.
And more hours work cleaning at the pub…

MAVIS. Him saving.

WENDELL. Saving far wha'?

WENDELL JUNIOR. I got go see Leon about this /

MAVIS. No. Not for now Junior. You going out too much these
days. I never know where to find you /

WENDELL JUNIOR. Me and my boys have ar squat.
That's where we spend most of our days.

But today we were mainly at the boys' club because today
they held a press conference…

Five days from now, the students are holding a march in
support. They've got people behind them now.

MAVIS. Who and what?

WENDELL JUNIOR. The bus boycott! They've officially
called for a boycott. Today May 1st. Today it has happened.
We can't ride the buses no more until they win.

MAVIS. Who *we*?

WENDELL JUNIOR. Black people. *Us*.

MAVIS. How am I meant to get up the hills by Totterdown?
I tried it once, and had to sit down halfway up.

Anyway none of these people forget the days that we have to
walk a whole hour to get to school. The bus system here like
a dream compared to that /

WENDELL JUNIOR. But Mummy you have to support.
  They're doing it for us too.

MAVIS. Is it?

WENDELL. Mi kyaan support son.

  Junior wha yuh say?

  Yuh an' yuh father united in the struggle?

  WENDELL JUNIOR *exits*.

Scene Two

St Agnes, Bristol. June 1963.

PRINCESS, *eyes closed, stands in the cupboard room.*
She is wearing a swimming costume and a sash around her.
She raises her hands in the air and places a crown made of
cardboard and tinsel on her head.

VOICE-OVER. *Ladies and gentlemen, I present to you the*
  winner of the year's Weston-super-Mare Beauties of the West
  Contest – (Voice booming.) Princess James.

  PRINCESS*'s eyes open wide.*
  The cupboard room explodes into a world of pageantry –
  seems less alive… still there… but somehow subdued.

  PRINCESS *approaches the microphone.*

PRINCESS. I…

  I…

  My name is Phyllis Princess James. I want to wear this
  crown…

  I want to be the prettiest girl in the whole of Weston-super-
  Mare and Bristol…

  But everyone in school says I can't be…

PRINCESS *picks up a small round mirror –*
She stares at her reflection in it –

Because…

PRINCESS *touches her lips –*

And my hair? And my skin is…

Beat.

Maybe I don't want to look like everyone else…

PRINCESS *hears a noise –*
The sound of a key turning in the door. The door opens –
PRINCESS *opens the door of the cupboard quietly –*
A light is switched on.

MAVIS *and* MARGOT *enter –* MARGOT *is shrieking with
laughter.*

MAVIS *tries to shush her quiet.*

WENDELL *follows quickly behind.*

They all seem a little bit tipsy.

MARGOT *almost falls over a large stack of packaged
toilet rolls.*

MAVIS. You trying to wake the whole building up Margot?

MARGOT. What are those?

WENDELL. What they look like?

MARGOT. Where you get those from Mavis?

WENDELL. Actually I bring them. I have a friend /

MARGOT. Just the one then!

MARGOT *laughs hard –*

MAVIS. Margot!

WENDELL. Mi providing far mi family anyway mi choose to.

MAVIS. My feet hurt so much. I'm sure they about to drop off.

MARGOT. But that was so much fun.

MAVIS. You gave them something to look at for certain.

MARGOT. Nevers seen Mavis enjoy herself so much.
     And those dance moves?
     Didn't think you had it in you.

MAVIS. These hips do more than push baby /

MARGOT. I nevers seen pushing like that before.

MAVIS. You want me to show you how?

     MAVIS *starts to whine her hips to imaginary music –*

     MARGOT *tries to imitate – badly –*

     WENDELL *sidles up to* MAVIS *– dancing close behind
     her –*

WENDELL. You see wha' dese Black wimmin kyaan do t'yuh!
     Dat's it baby /

     MAVIS *moves him away from him –*

MAVIS. All women know how to get a man to do things /

WENDELL. Is it?

MARGOT. I think I was getting plenty of attention myself.
     Dint you see?
     All sorts of attempts to you know...

WENDELL. Yuh making plenty attempts yuh self.
     No place safe fram de white woman *attempts*.

MARGOT. What you say?

WENDELL. De club welcome everybody for sure.

     Only inna Bristol yuh see so many different different people
     in same place.

MARGOT. Nearly danced until I broke my back mind /

WENDELL. I'm surprised yuh mout nuh pain yuh too.
     De way yuh chat chat to every person like...

MARGOT. Like what?

WENDELL. Well like yuh nuh know how to behave round people sometimes.

MAVIS. We had a nice evening.
Let's not spoil it /

MARGOT. I am a very friendly person if you must know.

WENDELL. Especially with de Black man it seem /

MARGOT. That being the only men available in there.
I play with the hands I got if you gets what I mean like.

WENDELL. No mi nuh *gets* it.

MARGOT. Well you clearly not shy with the white woman...

WENDELL. Dere go dat mouth again.

Wan-time fool no fool, but two-time fool damn fool!

MAVIS. Wendell!

Another drink Margot?

WENDELL. Tink *she* might need to be getting back.

MARGOT. No ways.

What you got?
More of that dark rum?
Might help to loosen these hips mind.

MAVIS. You going to make it back upstairs?

MARGOT. Might pass out on your sofa /

WENDELL. Mi carry yuh out if mi 'ave to.

MAVIS *hands* MARGOT *a glass of rum* –

MARGOT. You got enough of them eyes on you in there too Mavis.
A few men in there who wouldn't have minded having a dance /

WENDELL. *She* ar married woman!

MARGOT. Lighten up Wendell.

MAVIS. I don't care who's watching.

Since that place open last year, I just put it down as a place of sin.

But you know I might actually go back.

How you get to hear about that place Wendell?

WENDELL. Mi kyaant tell yuh dat...

WENDELL *taps his nose* –

MARGOT. Hustler by name.

Hustler by nature /

WENDELL. Wha' yuh know 'bout dat?

Yuh see mi in de days when mi hustle proper?

Take de clothes fram ya back an' yuh still be standing dere naked askin' how dat come t'be.

Slicker dan oil.

Faster dan lightning.

Hustle ar man outta 'im own witout breaking ar sweat!

Enuff story to tell.

MARGOT. Don't sound like nothing to be proud of if you asks me.

Taking what's not yours. Got another word for that /

MAVIS. That's the old Wendell /

WENDELL. Mi nuh play like dat no more.

Beat.

MAVIS. Been a long time since I dance like that.

And with *my* people.

WENDELL. It juss make mi happy to see yuh like it Mavis.

MARGOT. We could go back now.

It's still going.

Come on Mavis.

You know you wants to.

WENDELL. Mavis got ar lot to be doing tomorrow so /

MAVIS. Tomorrow is Sunday.

WENDELL. Yes an' de struggle nuh 'ave nuh days off.

MARGOT. What struggle?
No one going to be hiring tomorrow.
A day of rest.
For me head anyways.

WENDELL. Mi involved inna bigger fight now.
Bigger dan five pounds of Queen's money.
I tink dem boys wit de buses got something 'bout right /

MARGOT. You mean that silly bus-boycott lot?
In the papers making all sorts of accusations.
It's not like that here.
No reason to take it personal like.
You just have to accept how things are.

WENDELL. Nuh reason?

Nuh eberyting dat 'ave sugar sweet.

Yuh mean to tell mi when even ar Boys' Brigade officer nuh
get ar job cus 'im colour is far no good reason?

MAVIS. Margot don't mean it like that /

MARGOT. Yes I do.
There are some good people here.

You want things to change then you do it peaceful and all.
People trying to get along with each other.
Nobody wants that kind of trouble round here.

WENDELL. Wi see 'bout dat.
Yuh know de man running things in de boycott Paul
Stephenson?
'Im born here.
Dis country belong to alla us.

MARGOT. Hold on a minute.
People haves to be accommodated that's for sure, and many
people round here doing their best to be tolerating of youse,
and your West Indian churches, and you've got to be mindful
of *us*.

WENDELL. Wi done being mindful /

MARGOT. Not sure that's a good idea.

And no one going to be thanking you when you start taking away their overtime by giving work to them who never really...

Well...

My brother Dan. Other brother. Not that one married to that mouthy cow. The other one. Lives down by Bedminster. He been working on them buses since he come out of school. He's a good sort. A proper worker. Fixed your door lock dinned he when you couldn't find your keys 'member? Good laugh too. He works on them buses. I don't want to see him out of work cos of all this raucous...

Beat.

You got any more of this rum. Bloody delicious it is /

MAVIS. You want to drink me dry?

Anyway my legs feel like two piece ar dead wood. I'm going to go...

Margot you let yourself out.

WENDELL. Mavis wi only juss start...

MAVIS *exits.*

Beat.

MARGOT *pours herself another large glass of rum – which she downs in one mouthful –*

Tink yuh need to slow down.

MARGOT. Don't worry about me love.
Margot Barker not your average woman.

Can drink and talk anyones under the table.

WENDELL. Like yuh an' dat mouth running all over tings you know nuffin 'bout?

Beat.

MARGOT. Look 'ere!
    Don't get me wrong.
    You're alright.
    I mean I know you.
    I knows many of your lot.
    Makes no difference to me.
    But some of them men depend on those overtime hours.
    And you start giving those hours to other people, foreigners
    like, then well it's not going to go down well is it?

WENDELL. An' what 'bout de men dat need to feed deer
    children too?
    Do right far deer families.
    Make deer women proud.
    Have enuff spare change to treat dem like queens once in
    ar while.

MARGOT. Queens?!
    There's only one Queen in this country.

    MARGOT *laughs out loud* –

    There's other jobs.
    Better suited to them /

WENDELL. It driving damn buses.
    Who nuh suit dat?

    Yuh tink it juss de buses? De police, de fire brigade, de NHS
    dey all discriminating. When de last time yuh see somebody
    brown inna senior position inna hospital or classroom?

MARGOT. Don't shoot the messenger.

WENDELL. Yuh nuh messenger. Yuh juss anodder white
    woman trowing herself where she nuh wanted.

MARGOT. Them Liverpool ladies certainly got you all riled up.

WENDELL. Wha' yuh know 'bout Liverpool?

MARGOT. Mavis tells me everything. Like family I am.

    And they abouts the only family I've got so...

And I gets to walk in parts of the city others can't cus
everyone round here knows how close we are. Walk into any
church I like on any Sunday. I don't. But I could if I ever
wants to.

WENDELL. Mi see it all before Margot.
Yuh nuffin special.
As stale as de week's bread.
Happy to be seen wit ar nigger.
Even do de missionary ting for ar nigger but when it come
down to it Margot, yuh always stand by yuh own.

Yuh think mi lie?

MARGOT. Suit yourself.
Only trying to say it as it is.

We'll all be using the buses next week as usual.

But I tell you what Mavis don't need none of this. She has
taken to walking everywhere. Like she hasn't got enough on
her plate, now she's walking back and forth to show *support*.

She could do without the troubles you lot bringing. She's a
good sort and not one to rock the boat that brought her here.

And you do good to remember that Wendell James.

WENDELL *kisses his teeth –*

Now to top up that beauty sleep!

MARGOT *grabs a pack of toilet roll – and exits.*

WENDELL *stands shaking his head after* MARGOT *–*

MAVIS *enters.*

WENDELL. Dat woman!

If speech wort shillin, silence worth pound!

MAVIS. Quiet down Wendell! She's just got a big mouth, but
she innocent really.

And my head paining real bad now /

WENDELL. Saying what everybody else tinks.

Mavis, mi kyaant leave dis alone.

Now dem man Roy Hackett an' Paul Stephenson announce
de bus boycott it all going to get very interesting. Wi 'ave to
do everything wi kyaan.

Tomorra mi knocking on every door an' church of every
Black person inna Bristol telling dem 'bout dis situation.
Giving leaflet. Tarking 'bout the real struggle.
Educate dem.

MAVIS *moves to stand close to* WENDELL –

Dis is serious tings Mavis.

De unions, all of dem dey 'ave to answer far dis colour bar.
Dey 'ave ta answer to us far taking food outta children mouth.
Dey 'ave ta!

Beat.

MAVIS. You make me proud 'usband.

WENDELL. It sweet to hear yuh call mi yuh 'usband again.
Yuh mean dat Mavis?

Beat.

MAVIS. Yes.

WENDELL. An' mi get all de rights of ar husband too?

MAVIS. I can't think what rights you talking about?

MAVIS *and* WENDELL *are now playing a game of cat and
mouse around the table* –

WENDELL. I mean de rights ar man might 'ave if 'im find
'imself inna de marital bed.

MAVIS. Who say anything about a bed?
Not everything 'ave ta happen inna bed.

WENDELL *bites his hand with frustration* –

WENDELL. Where?…
Mi mean…
How…
Yuh playing wit mi Mavis James?

MAVIS *stops running –*

WENDELL *moves to stand face to face with* MAVIS *–*

Beat.

MAVIS. Why don't you turn off the lights and I tell you?

WENDELL. Sweet Jesus.
  Tank you!

  WENDELL *slaps* MAVIS *on backside again –*

  MAVIS *giggles –*

  PRINCESS *closes the door to the cupboard again –*
  She sits with her back firmly against the door –
  Sighs heavily –

Scene Three

St Agnes, Bristol. June 1963.

The room is filled with boxes labelled – 'Broken Biscuits'.

MAVIS, WENDELL, PRINCESS *and* LORNA *are sitting on the sofas and armchairs.*

MAVIS *is plaiting* PRINCESS's *hair.*

WENDELL *is reading a newspaper.*

LORNA *is playing with a doll.*

WENDELL. Dem really showing themselves up now.
  Can't believe wha' my man here saying 'bout de bus boycott.
  Wait…
  Let mi juss read yuh ar lickle section of dis –

  Beat.

  '*It is true that London Transport employ a large coloured staff… As a result of this, the amount of white labour dwindles steadily on the London Underground. You won't get*

a white man in London to admit it, but which of them will
join a service where they may find themselves working under
a coloured foreman?... I understand that in London,
coloured men have become arrogant and rude, after they
have been employed for some months.'

Yuh hear that? Arrogant and rude 'pparently.
Wha' good enough far London Transport nuh good nuff far
de Bristol Omnibus Company.

Even when Tony Benn an' Harold Wilson 'emselves
speaking against dere actions, dey still feel to tark like dis?
Dey fine far our cricketers to come 'ere to de County Ground
an' play *Gloucestershire* but no one wan' to be giving deer
bus change to nuh Black man.

MAVIS. I pick up something today...

MAVIS *reaches for a folded newspaper in her bag –*

This one woman write...
Wait let me find it...

A Bristol woman, Mrs Margaret Batt, write to the newspaper,
all the way from Jamaica just to say –

'*Is this the example which Britain is set to other*
Commonwealth countries and to the rest of the world?
Is our criticism of South Africa's policy, in these
circumstances, not merely a case of "the kettle calling the
pan sooty"?'

You see how people supporting? /

LORNA. Daddy can I go and see Margot?

WENDELL. Dat woman ignorant!

MAVIS. Not now Lorna.

LORNA. I want to say thank you for my doll.
She gave it to me yesterday.
Because my hair is as pretty as a doll's she said /

WENDELL. She 'ave ar lot to say 'bout ar lot of tings.

PRINCESS. Is my hair pretty too Mummy?

LORNA. She said she's going to do them into ringlets for me. Nice like t' other girls at school.

WENDELL (*to* MAVIS). You still tink she *juss tarking*? Mi feel ar way 'bout how she talk an' mi nuh sure at all 'bout giving har any time wit mi darters.

PRINCESS. Mummy!

MAVIS. Wendell!

WENDELL. Wi tark 'bout dis already Mavis.

WENDELL *stares hard at* MAVIS –

It decided. Yuh girls nuh go to har place. She nuh look after dem again. Fram now if mi or yuh modder not here, den she nuh allowed inna dis house. She nuh welcome yuh hear?

PRINCESS *slumps in a sulk –*
WENDELL JUNIOR *enters. He is bleeding and hurt – stumbling –*
WENDELL *jumps to his feet – runs to catch him –*
MAVIS *runs to the kitchen to grab a towel –*

Wha' 'appen Junior?
Wha' dis?

WENDELL JUNIOR. –

MAVIS. Junior say something? You been fighting?

WENDELL JUNIOR *shakes his head –*

What then?

WENDELL. Yuh badly hurt son? It hurting anywhere in particular?

WENDELL JUNIOR *shakes his head –*

MAVIS. Who do this?

PRINCESS *runs to hold* WENDELL JUNIOR *tightly around the leg.*

PRINCESS. Poor Junior. I have plasters Junior.
You want my plasters?

WENDELL *bats* PRINCESS *away – She stands close –*

WENDELL JUNIOR. They jumped us in town.There was
another march. For the boycott. A bigger one for students.
We were running late and couldn't make it up to the
Suspension Bridge so met them at the bottom of Park Street.
So many people. Walking proud. Students all shouting – '*No
to the colour bar. Not in our name.*' It felt good. No trouble
really. The bus crews were there. All shouting too. But they
were outnumbered. Fair and square. More of us than them
this time. People tearing up their bus tickets.
Then on the way back to the squat...

MAVIS. I don't like this squat business /

WENDELL. Dat nuh matter far now.

WENDELL JUNIOR. We see four white boys. Big. Ugly.
Standing on the corner by the Chocolate Factory. They
follow us. We try to pretend they're not there but by the time
we get to the cemetery, they're real close. Come right close
up to us. Then they start pushing and shoving. And then
more of them turn up. Pushing harder...
Saying their daddies work for the buses and don't want no
coloured bastards working with them.

WENDELL. Dey do dis to yuh? Laid ar hand 'pon mi own?

WENDELL JUNIOR. They got as good as they gave. If it
weren't for the bicycle chains /

WENDELL. Bicycle chain! Dat nuh right at all. Beat up like dis
far standing up far good? Far de right ting?
Mi going to find de devil chile an' give dem ar beating. Mi
done wit dese bakra!

WENDELL *exits.*

MAVIS. Wendell!

MAVIS *runs after him – only as far as the door –*

WENDELL JUNIOR *walks dejected to his room* – MAVIS
anxiously follows him –

PRINCESS. Will we get beat up too?
　　Maybe we won't go out again.
　　We'll have to hide in here forever.

LORNA. I'm not going to hide.
　　I'm not like *you*.

PRINCESS. If I get beat up so do you!
　　Let's hide!

　　PRINCESS *attempts to take* LORNA*'s hand* –

　　LORNA *pulls away hard* –

LORNA. I won't get beat up.

PRINCESS. But we're sisters /

LORNA. I'm not Black like you.
　　I'm only half.
　　Half of everything.
　　Half-sister.
　　Half-caste.
　　Everyone says so.

　　MAVIS *looks up* –

I don't want a sister.
I want my mum.
I want to go home!

　　LORNA *runs off – exits*.

　　MAVIS *runs to* PRINCESS *who is standing in the middle of
　　the room. Holds her tighter than she's ever held her before.*

Scene Four

St Agnes, Bristol. July 1963.

MAVIS, *with music in the background, folds clothes. Meditatively taking them from the clothes dryer precariously standing in the middle of the room, folding them, and placing them in a basket next to her.*

MARGOT *enters. She stares hard at the boxes that seem to be taking up more space in the kitchen.*

MARGOT. There you are!

MAVIS. Yes.

MARGOT. Haven't seen you for while…

> *Beat.*

> Starting to think you're avoiding me.

MAVIS. I've been busy.

> *Beat.*

MARGOT. New radio?

> MAVIS *turns music off –*

MAVIS. Yes. Wendell knows a man at the market who gets the latest models /

MARGOT. He bought it did he?

MAVIS. It was a gift. He knows how much I like to listen to the wireless.

> *Beat.*

MARGOT. I've been round asking after you /

MAVIS. What they do to Junior…
He's just a boy!

MARGOT. There's a lot of bad feeling at the moment. If Wendell hadn't brought all this talk /

MAVIS. People looking at me a bit stranger in those houses these days. I see something different in them eyes.

MARGOT. That's what's I'm saying. Wendell and those *others* stirring it. Stirring it up and /

MAVIS. It's not Wendell's fault that the world look at us like we lesser. Look at us somehow as second-class citizens. This country call upon us to work. Call us! And now we're here they're telling us only certain work suit us. Who do you think runs the hospitals and schools in the Caribbean?

MARGOT. This is what I mean. He has everyone singing out of his songbook now.

I need a cuppa!

MARGOT *moves to the kitchen to fill the kettle –*

MAVIS. I'm busy Margot…

MARGOT. He wormed his way into your bed again is that it?

MAVIS. Margot! You know that I don't discuss things like that /

MARGOT. I just want to know Mavis. I wants to know if I'm no longer welcome here now…

It's no secret that my life isn't exactly a shining example of anything worthwhile. A woman in her… widow even… in her early thirties… living independently with the best curves this side of Bristol… is something *rare*. I know. But it gets lonely up there in that flat. And if it weren't for them babbers… cos you know I sees them as my own… if it weren't for them and you…

I mean I don'ts like to be where I'm not wanted…

MAVIS. It's…

Things get a little complex…

Wendell he is…

MARGOT. Why is he still here Mavis?

Why you listening to all his speeches about this bus and that union and…

And I've been hearing things around…

MAVIS. We have never exchanged a bad word between us
Margot but you have to stop talking like this.

Certain things I never told you Margot about my life with
him before. Sometimes I don't recognise the woman wearing
these clothes. Most days in fact…

MAVIS *takes a seat –*

MARGOT *busies herself with making a pot of tea –*

You know something Margot? All those years ago, we were
young and happy. I knew from the beginning what he was.
My mother said it. His mother said it. The whole town was
saying it –

*Dat bwoy ar hustler! 'Im nevar earn ar honest day's money
in 'im life!*

But then he goes into the service. And whenever I see him on
leave, he look so sharp. Uniform straight. Hair combed.
Taking me out proper.

After a few years, he was discharged after an incident
because as they examine him they find he have a condition.
Something on his lung they said. Well he come back to
Jamaica but they promise him a desk job. A good job in
Hingland if he want it. We get married on April 1st 1945.
April Fools' Day. Imagine! But I was already carrying Junior
by the time we arrive in England.

MARGOT *places two cups of tea on the table –*
She sits too –

I feel so lucky Margot. A husband with a job, a baby and this
new land of Hope and Glory. 'Cept you see when we move
here to Hingland we didn't find no hope that for sure.

Wendell arrives at the place to work, they tell him to start as
a junior clerk. He was a second lieutenant back home, and
had never done an office job in his life. He didn't understand
why they invite him to come here if all they want to do is
make him feel invisible.

So just like that things change. He give up on the job. Take to staying out all hours of the night. And I was stuck here with Junior. And no way of knowing what he was doing. But people start talking...

I nagged. I controlled. I made sure he didn't make a move without me knowing. I used to have people report on 'im if they see him where he shouldn't be. I thought I was getting through.

But The Hustler was back. Lying. Scheming...

And when he left. Disappeared just like that one night. I cry of course! Cry like I never cry before. Then...

MAVIS *takes a sip of tea –*

I start to feel something different. Like a kind of... like something lift off my shoulders. Like a kind of freedom.

MARGOT. And now? You still got that feeling Mavis?

MAVIS. All I know is everything harder when you try to change a man.

MARGOT. So you're going to just let him get away with anything he wants to?

MAVIS. He is trying to make good with this bus action.

MARGOT. You really believe that?

MAVIS. Only so many battles I can fight Margot.
I want to survive long enough for my children to feel like this their home too.
That's all I have the strength for these days.

MARGOT. And what if nothing comes of the bus boycott? What then Mavis? Think he's still going to be a changed man?

MAVIS *looks away from* MARGOT –

MAVIS. If a whole city can try to change, why not one simple man?

MARGOT *puts her cup down –*

MARGOT. So that's it is it? That's the way /

MAVIS. Yes.

Beat.

MAVIS *puts the radio back on –*
The radio signal crackles and then cuts out –

MARGOT. I'll see you then. Mavis…

MAVIS *doesn't look up –*

MARGOT *exits.*

Scene Five

St Agnes, Bristol. 24 August 1963.

WENDELL JUNIOR *is sitting at the kitchen table in front of*
a dismantled camera, meticulously cleaning it.

PRINCESS *lies on the sofa – a blanket almost covering her*
entire head and face.

WENDELL *enters from the front door –*
He moves to kitchen sink –

WENDELL. Mawnin' son.

Mi an' yuh modder take ar lickle early-morning walk up to
some big house in Clifton. She nuh take de bus now. Mi an'
she walk all dat way juss to measure up dem curtains.

Yuh see dem houses? Mi kyannt imagine any amount of
fabric big enuff far dem windows. Yuh modder say it simpler
– '*Dem need to be sure dey kyaant see de poor fram dem big*
winda.'

Beat.

Yuh doing ar fine job wit dat camera.

WENDELL JUNIOR. Princess sick with something…

WENDELL. Still?

> WENDELL *walks over to the sofa and peers at* PRINCESS
> *who lies motionless –*
> *He moves to kitchen cupboard, pulls out bottle and pours*
> *himself a drink –*

Medicine.

> WENDELL *takes a seat at the table opposite –*

Yuh make mi proud son.
Prouder dan ar cockerel.
De way yuh focus so hard on yuh photography.

WENDELL JUNIOR. So you're not going to get a job?

WENDELL. Yes yes! Once mi give everything mi got to dis
boycott action /

WENDELL JUNIOR. Most people managing to keep a job, and
help out with the boycott /

WENDELL. Most people nuh mi! Mi put mi heart full into
everything. Mi hundred per cent committed to see dem men
dere inna bus-company uniform looking sharp like razor
blade!

Yuh nuh let ar few bruises stop yuh! Wi 'ava fight far
equality. Nothing come far free /

WENDELL JUNIOR. Mummy works every day for things to
be free /

WENDELL. Mi de man of dis house an' dat de way de stay now!

Yuh do better to adjust yuh attitude Junior. Make it easier far
all us to be ar family again.

> WENDELL JUNIOR *moves towards his room and exits –*

> PRINCESS *who has had her eyes open, listening, quickly*
> *shuts them again –*

Junior! Dis bwoy testing every inch of mi soul!

WENDELL JUNIOR *enters. He is holding a bag. He puts the bag on the table and pushes it towards* WENDELL.

WENDELL JUNIOR. Have it!

WENDELL *peers into the bag –*

I know you think you're going to *stay*. That things are different and that you are different…

WENDELL. Where yuh get dis?

WENDELL JUNIOR. There's enough there for you and Lorna to find somewhere to live. Outside Bristol. Back to Liverpool or… anywhere! Twenty pounds all yours.

I can get more. Or borrow some from Leon /

WENDELL. Junior think straight /

WENDELL JUNIOR. All you have to do is leave. Just leave.

WENDELL. You really think? /

WENDELL JUNIOR. I'll leave it here. For you. I've got to go to work now…

WENDELL JUNIOR *extends his hand waiting for a handshake –*

Have a good life!

WENDELL JUNIOR *heads towards door –*

WENDELL. Yuh feel real hate far mi like dis?

WENDELL JUNIOR. I remember hearing her crying. Every day and every night after you left. It was like some kind of sad song, no more could turn off. It went on forever and I thought it was never going to stop. But it did. One day it did. That one day Princess was walking around the kitchen with a pan on her head, hitting it with a stick and dancing to her own music like she didn't know it was her making it. And I remember Mummy laughed. For the first time, I heard her laugh. We all laughed. It was like a new song being played for the first time.

I don't hate you. I just love them more. And Princess…

WENDELL. Dat girl love me. An' she love har sister same way /

WENDELL JUNIOR. She wouldn't have recognised you a few weeks ago /

WENDELL. Yuh wan' do dat to dem? Yuh baby sisters?

WENDELL JUNIOR *exits.*

WENDELL *stands looking at the bag on the table. He puts his hand in and holds up a single note to the light. He looks harder inside the bag. He shuts the bag tight and exits to other room.*

PRINCESS *opens one eye but before she can move,* WENDELL *appears out of the bedroom without the bag.* PRINCESS *quickly closes eyes again.*

WENDELL *puts his hat and coat on – exits.*

PRINCESS *sits up immediately –*

PRINCESS. Baby? I am not a baby!

PRINCESS *moves a drawer – opens it and takes out a pair of tailor's scissors – too big for her small hands. She walks to her cupboard – but now her world of pageantry doesn't come alive. Instead we see it for just what it is. A dark room, strewn with mop and bucket, brooms and other rejected items from the household. On the walls and ceiling hangs a variety of handmade art and decorations.*

I am Phyllis. I am Phyllis James.

PRINCESS *stands for a beat, feeling more alone than ever. She picks up costumes/dress from her box and starts to cut up them up. She kicks and screams – and destroys her cupboard world.*

PRINCESS *leaves the cupboard – she walks to where* WENDELL*'s hat is hanging and picks it up. She exits into the bedroom – hat and scissors in hand.*

ACT THREE

Scene One

St Agnes, Bristol. 24 August 1963. Evening.

MAVIS *stands in the middle of the living room, clearly distressed.*

WENDELL JUNIOR *and* LEON *enter.*

MAVIS. Junior! Where you been till this time?

WENDELL JUNIOR. Sorry Mummy. I was just...

I got some extras shifts at the warehouse.

MAVIS. Is your sister with you? Have you seen your father?

WENDELL JUNIOR. No. What's happened?

MAVIS. Your sister's gone. I've been up and down those streets twenty times /

WENDELL JUNIOR. Have you tried Margot's she's always there dressing up if she's not here /

MAVIS. She's not there! I've been knocking on Margot's door every half-hour since I come back and found Princess gone /

LEON. What about Mr James, won't she be with him?

MAVIS. He wouldn't take her out, she's sick. She's barely moved off that chair for the past week. And I find this...

MAVIS *pulls out several locks of* PRINCESS*'s hair from a waste bin.*

I've got a bad feeling about this.

Leon, will you stay here and mind Lorna for me?

LEON. Yes Mrs James of course.

MAVIS. She won't be any bother, she's fast asleep, tired out from all that marching up and down with me all afternoon.

MAVIS *heads for the door –*

LEON. I'm sure Princess is fine. She's probably someplace playing her Princess thing.

MAVIS. Thank you Leon. Junior we've got to find her. You walk towards the city centre and I'll go and try Margot again. Oh Lord, please look after my baby.

WENDELL JUNIOR *doesn't move –*

Junior! What are you waiting on? Your sister needs you!

WENDELL JUNIOR. Daddy. I told him to go. I gave him all my savings and I told him to go.

MAVIS. What you say? Why would you do such a thing? Junior?

WENDELL JUNIOR. I told him to take Lorna I didn't think he'd…

MAVIS. You didn't think! And now your sister gone someplace and /

WENDELL JUNIOR. But he's showed his true colours now hasn't he?

LEON. Junior! Mrs James, Junior doesn't mean it.

WENDELL JUNIOR. Yes I do. He's gone like I said he would /

LEON. Mr James could come back with Princess any minute. He's probably out collecting signatures for the petition again, you know what he's like. You'll see.

MAVIS. Yes, I know what he's like.

MAVIS *turns and looks at the hat stand, and sees* WENDELL*'s hat has gone.*

WENDELL JUNIOR. You've still got me. I will never leave you.

MAVIS. We have to find your sister. I can't lose my Princess. My joy.

MAVIS *exits.*

Scene Two

St Agnes, Bristol. 24 August 1963. Even later that evening.

MARGOT *enters her small bedsit room. It is dark until she fumbles and finds a light.*
She closes the door. She leans against the door for a beat. She moves to a dresser a few feet away, looks at herself in the dresser mirror, and slowly peels off her earrings, rings and eyelashes. She takes off her bra – expertly doing whilst keeping her dress in place, and slides a wig off her head. Her limp and lacklustre hair underneath falls to her shoulders. She looks at herself again. Pauses. She hears something. Pauses. Picks up a shoe.

MARGOT. Someone in 'ere? Someone trying to play games with me? I've got a gun 'ere mind and I can use it. I'll use it to blow your blimming head off. I'm not some scuttler youse hear?

Come out!

A rustle by the side of the bed –

Beat.

PRINCESS *slowly appears from her hiding place –*
Her hair is cut short and uneven –

Princess!

MARGOT *throws shoe back on the floor –*

Babber what you think you're doing sneaking in 'ere?
Did you get the spare key outta the kitchen drawer? Your ma's going to flip her lid.

You nearly gave me a blimming heart attack. You want to have that on your conscience for the rest of your life? How you get in 'ere?

Beat.

What the bloody hell's happened to your hair? Princess?

MARGOT *turns on another side lamp –*

Say something then!

Beat.

Your ma know you're 'ere Princess?

PRINCESS *shakes her head –*

Sit on the bed. Sit there whiles I put my wig back on and get you along to yours /

PRINCESS. No! I want to stay with you Margot.

I have run away!

MARGOT. Run away? Ark at ee!

What's there to be running away from? And where's you planning on going? Your escape? Where's that to then?

PRINCESS *bursts into tears –*

MARGOT *runs to hug the sobbing* PRINCESS –

Princess no one's running anywhere!

MARGOT *places* PRINCESS *back on the bed, and sits down next to her –*

MARGOT *goes to a small cupboard/wardrobe and starts to rummage –*

MARGOT *emerges with a bright-blue dress in her hands –*

How do you fancy wearing a ball gown to bed tonight? It's an old one. Don't wear it any more what with it reminding me of my Fred.

Tomorrow you will be back at school running around the playground with your friends playing Hopscotch /

PRINCESS. They say mean things to me.
They only like Lorna now.
They tell me to go away.
Go back to where I came from.

What does that mean?

MARGOT. Is that what all this is about Princess?

PRINCESS. I don't want no beauty pageants or Weston-super-Mare. I don't care if I don't see the donkeys or eat choc ices... but I can imagine they are delicious... but...

Please run away with me Margot. Lorna says she won't tell anyone.
Will you? If you don't I'll have to go on my own and /

MARGOT. And how am I going to go to Weston-super-Mare without my Princess? Without the prettiest girl in all of Bristol.

PRINCESS. Mummy won't be happy now /

MARGOT. All your ma wants is for *you* to be happy. You've got lots of growing up to do before you need to worry /

PRINCESS. I thought if I was a beauty queen, and I won the prize money then I could buy anything I wanted. And I would buy my mummy a big house. That will make her happy. A big house with the best curtains. But I can't be can I... I can't win!

MARGOT. Everything will be just fine Princess.

PRINCESS. I want her to have her big house and happiness now!

MARGOT. *Now* is bedtime.

Beat.

PRINCESS. You look different Margot.

What happened to *your* hair?

MARGOT. I'm old. That's what. Old with all sorts of new tricks...

Now you gets to sleep...

No more of this running-away talk.

PRINCESS *slips out of her dress and into the oversized ball gown –*
MARGOT *then tucks her up in her bed –*

PRINCESS. Are you not going to sleep too Margot?

MARGOT. Yes I am. And I'm going to be sleeping right next to my Princess and keep her safe.

First I've just got a little errand to run before I gets in. So you just close your eyes…

PRINCESS, *exhausted, closes her eyes happily – and goes to sleep –*
MARGOT *watches* PRINCESS *for a moment, making sure she's really asleep –*

(*Whispering.*) Poor little chicken! Think I'm going to have to pop upstairs and let 'em know where you are… Mavis will be at her wits' end by now. Everything will be right as rain tomorrow.

Everything will be right as rain tomorrow. I promise you Princess.

MARGOT *exits.*

Scene Three

St Agnes, Bristol. 25 August 1963.

MAVIS *sits, pretending to be sewing some curtains.*

WENDELL JUNIOR *is hanging developed pictures on a string across the room.*
LORNA *is reading a book.*

Music is playing.

A key turns in door.

PRINCESS *and* MARGOT *enter.* PRINCESS *is wearing a wide-brimmed hat.*

MARGOT *takes a look round – sighing at the thought that what was once familiar no longer feels like hers.*

MAVIS *jumps up out of her seat and wraps her arms around* PRINCESS.

MAVIS. Princess!

WENDELL JUNIOR. Princess what were you thinking?

PRINCESS. Mummy. I'm sorry I ran away /

MAVIS. Why would you want to do that Princess?

MARGOT. She's been helping me out /

MAVIS. Margot...

MARGOT *straightens up* –

MARGOT. You alright Mavis?

Beat.

MARGOT *spots the pictures hanging up* –

Always knew you was talented Junior but these...

Beautiful people.

There's one of you here Princess. 'My Sister, The Beauty Queen'.

PRINCESS *walks to stare at the image of herself. Sash on. Crown on* –

Beat.

Princess is just fine.

MAVIS. I need to talk to *my* children Margot.

PRINCESS. But Mummy it was Margot that looked after me /

MARGOT *heads for the front door* –

MARGOT. It's alright Mavis. I gets it.

PRINCESS. Don't go Margot!

MARGOT *stops – stands awkwardly by the door* –

LORNA. Am I in any of them Junior?

WENDELL JUNIOR *points at another one of the images hanging up* –

WENDELL JUNIOR. That one's called 'My Other Sister'.

LORNA *smiles a big smile* –

LORNA (*to* PRINCESS). Where's my daddy?

PRINCESS *shrugs* –

MAVIS. It doesn't matter for now. We have each other /

LORNA. When's he coming back?

MAVIS. Your daddy might be gone somewhere /

PRINCESS. Is Lorna going to have to go away too?

MAVIS. No Princess. We are all going to stay right here. This is where we belong and your daddy… he's got to find where he belongs.

PRINCESS. Margot here's your hat back.

PRINCESS *takes the hat off* –

MAVIS. Princess James!
Lawd a mercy! What 'appened to yuh hair?

WENDELL JUNIOR. That is really…

MAVIS. Which devil throw scissors 'pon yuh head dis way? Margot you do this?

PRINCESS. I…

LORNA. I think I like it Princess /

WENDELL JUNIOR. I mean it's a look!

WENDELL JUNIOR *tries to hide his laughter* –

MAVIS. None of this is funny! Let me go get some kind of comb to do something with this…

MARGOT. Mavis. I don't like to speak out of turn because well I'm brought up proper, and ladies like me, we know how to stay well out of things…
Anyways I just wants you to be happy… remember that. You know where I am if you need me.

You keep the hat Princess…

I've got a couple of errands need doing.

MAVIS. Thank you for bringing Princess back home safe to me. And you're always welcome here. Any time. Girls say bye to your Auntie Margot.

The girls turn to MARGOT –

PRINCESS *and* LORNA. Bye Auntie Margot!

A tear runs down MARGOT*'s cheek – she wipes her eyes – and exits quickly.*

MAVIS. Lorna, Princess you two go wash your hands ready for food. Think we all need a good meal after all these *surprises*.

PRINCESS *and* LORNA *exeunt.*

MAVIS *moves to the kitchen and starts to cook dinner for her children.*

Scene Four

St Agnes, Bristol. 28 August 1963.

WENDELL *staggering – enters.*

WENDELL (*shouting*). Mavis!
Mi 'ave tings to be celebrating… get some news …
Mavis!
Today is ar new day!

MAVIS *enters.*

WENDELL *staggers towards her –*

MAVIS. Shhhh!!…
So you're here…

WENDELL. Where else?

MAVIS. You haven't come home for a whole two days Wendell! What you think we all doing here? And what you think Princess and Lorna thinking now?

WENDELL. Exactly! Two 'hol' days mi missing in action! But lissen to mi now Mavis /

MAVIS. No you listen! You cannot start this… this… disappearing act with me again you hear!

Take your bag and stay out. Get out Wendell James. Get out for good!

PRINCESS *opens the door from the bedroom* – LORNA *and* WENDELL JUNIOR *follow* –
WENDELL JUNIOR *holds his sisters close* –

MAVIS *and* WENDELL *do not see them standing there* –

WENDELL. Dat wha' mi wan' tell yuh Mavis! Dem two days mi have some serious things 'appen /

WENDELL JUNIOR *lets go of his sisters* – *moves towards* WENDELL –

WENDELL JUNIOR. Why are you back?
You said /

WENDELL. I never say anything /

WENDELL JUNIOR. You're not wanted here /

WENDELL. Dat between mi an' yuh modder son.

WENDELL JUNIOR. You thief!

WENDELL. Hol' up! Who yuh calling teef? Mi nuh teef any ting in mi 'hol' life!

WENDELL JUNIOR. You took that money and you're still here! I told you to take it and leave but you're still here and now you're /

WENDELL. Mi nuh take nuh money. Mi never touch it! In fack /

WENDELL JUNIOR. That was my money! My money for when I get an apprenticeship! I've been saving that for nearly two years!
You're the worst father any family can ask for.

WENDELL JUNIOR *bursts into full tears* –

WENDELL *grips* WENDELL JUNIOR*'s arm hard –*

WENDELL. Hush up! Yes yuh leff dat money on de table. But mi put it right back where it belong. In yuh room. In it rightful place /

MAVIS. You don't touch *my* son.

WENDELL *lets go of* WENDELL JUNIOR*'s arm –*

WENDELL JUNIOR. See you're lying. You don't even know where I keep it.

WENDELL. Yuh sure 'bout that? Dey never call mi Hustler far nuh good reason.

WENDELL JUNIOR. So where is it then!

PRINCESS. It was Junior's money!

WENDELL. What yuh know about it Princess? Yuh lissenin' inna business nuh yuh own?

PRINCESS. I heard it all. You're going to take Junior's money, and run away from us... from me again. And you did run away, and Mummy has been crying, because, because...

PRINCESS *bursts into tears –*

WENDELL. Be quiet! Nuh more cryin' like a baby /

PRINCESS. I am not a baby! Junior is right about you. You're nothing but a hustler!

MARGOT *enters.*

MARGOT. Can hears youse all the way down the corridors /

WENDELL. Dis family business Margot so go home!

MARGOT. Rather wait... if alright with Mavis /

MAVIS. This my house and Margot stay as long as she want!

MARGOT. Actually Mavis. Not sure I've got time for tea or 'em dumpling thingies...
I'm going to the pictures. With a man!
Found this in my room and not ever seen it before so...

MARGOT *puts bag on the table –*

WENDELL JUNIOR *grabs the bag –*

You can thank me later.

WENDELL JUNIOR. How did it end up your room Margot?

MARGOT *exits.*

WENDELL. Well well. Mi nuhn out dat money dere so there must be another hustler in dis family here.

All eyes turn to PRINCESS –

WENDELL JUNIOR. Princess? Why?

PRINCESS. I…
I thought we could use it for the bus to Weston-super-Mare. Then we can all go /

WENDELL. That's what mi tryna tell you…

Beat.

Yesterday when mi leave 'ere, mi head over to one house where alla us boycott people gathering. Plenty of us dere. Nuh body really talking. Yuh see wi all dere waiting far de news. It quiet. Nuh body knowing wha' t'say. Dem bus workers 'ave ar meeting. Union come to tark.
Five hundred of dem all gathered inna some place tarking far hours…
The whole place filled with hope. Someting big coming. Mi feel it in mi bones. Something bigger than all our hopes. Dat where mi been. Dat what mi trying to say…

MAVIS *stands and moves over to an open window – she leans out – takes a deep breath –*

Yuh hear dat Mavis?
Wi might actually win dis ting.
Far once.
Wi take on de system an' it look like wi might beat dem.
Mi no lie Mavis.
And well mi 'ave ta 'ave ar lickle drink to celebrate dat, and well night turn till mawnin'…

WENDELL *takes a handkerchief from his pocket and wipes his eyes* –

Beat.

Nobody 'ave anything to say?

WENDELL JUNIOR. Wild…
Unbelievable…

MAVIS. Them actually going to let Black men work on the buses?

WENDELL. Yuh see dem men dat make dis happen, dem heroes. If this come off, it ar victory far de Black man. De brown man. Every kinda man dem.

PRINCESS. And girls and women!

WENDELL *goes over to the radio and turns it on loud –*
He dances to the music blaring out of it –
The children watch bemused but do not join in –
WENDELL *suddenly turns the music off –*

WENDELL. Lissen Mavis.
Mi an' yuh got tings to discuss /
Some tings kyannt wait yuh hear.

WENDELL *moves towards* MAVIS –
He circles her with one arm and plants a long kiss on her mouth –

Dere supm mi 'ave ta say Mavis.

MAVIS. Children go to your room!

PRINCESS. But Mummy /

MAVIS *gives her a hard look –*

PRINCESS *and* LORNA *exeunt.*

MAVIS. You too Junior. Go now…

WENDELL JUNIOR *stares at* WENDELL *hard –*
WENDELL JUNIOR *exits.*

MAVIS *turns her back on* WENDELL –

WENDELL. Yuh right Mavis...
Mi have plenty to explain mi know dat...
It juss ...
Mavis lissen up.

WENDELL *slowly lowers himself until he is on one bended knee –*

MAVIS *turns to face him –*

MAVIS. What are you doing?

WENDELL *reaches into his pocket and pulls out a ring –*
He holds it out towards MAVIS *–*

WENDELL. Mavis.
God muss 'ave known what 'im doing when he create yuh.
Yuh de best woman any man kyaan arsk far in 'im life.
Mi marry once but it feel to mi dat yuh ar woman dat need to
be respected so I juss wan' know if yuh do mi enuff honour
an' be mi wife far anodder time...

MAVIS *kisses her teeth –*

Wha' yuh say Mavis? Yuh going to make mi de happiest man
on dis God-given earth? Mi nuh take nuh far answer Mavis /

MAVIS. All this time I was thinking you...

Beat.

Mi 'ave dreams too Wendell. Small quiet dreams but dem
still alive in 'ere...
And every day, mawning and night mi fall on my knees and
pray that dis country Hingland truly see de possibilities of
our children... dat dem juss see dat...

WENDELL. Our children? You see mi involve in dem dreams
Mavis?

MAVIS. You just hear what you want to hear Wendell James.

Beat.

What you done to us cannot easily be forgiven Wendell and
you see these children, they the ones that need you to change.
Princess needs you to know all of her dreams, because they are

important. She needs to know that even when the world out there ready to break her heart, we in *here* never let it happen that way. And Junior... you need to teach him what a good man look like. If you can't do that, then better to leave now.

WENDELL. No mi hear you good. Because yuh see my children teach mi good. Something far mi to look up to. 'Im know if yuh wan' it den yuh 'ave ta work far it.
Mi see all our dreams coming together Mavis...
Hustle nuh win anything far mi. Mi see dat...

Beat.

Tomorrow morning mi heading straight to docks to ask far work.
Now mi 'ave ar family to look after...
Let mi go take ar wash. Den we kyaan tark...
Or yuh kyann tark an' mi juss lissen...

MAVIS. Hmm...

WENDELL *exits to bedroom.*

Scene Five

St Agnes, Bristol. 28 August 1963.

A short while later.

MAVIS *is dressed, ready to go out.*

MAVIS. Girls hurry up with putting your shoes on!

LORNA *enters.*
She is dressed elaborately in a dress from MARGOT*'s* –

Where's Princess?

I want us to be out there!

LORNA. She got dressed and went somewhere.

MAVIS. That girl stranger every day!

Where's your brother?

I don't have time for no dilly or dally from you children today.

Go get Junior!

LORNA *exits*.

Beat.

Come out of there Princess.
Princess Phyllis James do not make me come to look for you!

The cupboard door opens –
PRINCESS *pops her head from round the door –*

PRINCESS *watches her mother intensely as she steps out of the cupboard –*

MAVIS. Princess…

I can feel that thing you always talking about…

PRINCESS. Mummy…

MAVIS. Like someone take a whole hive fulla honey and pour it into me!

PRINCESS. Like when my dreams fill me up. Fill everything up…

MAVIS. Yes just like that…

PRINCESS. I don't feel it any more Mummy. I don't think I can be pretty again. Ever. Now my hair is like this and /

MAVIS. What you say? Phyllis James you listen, and you listen good!
Whether your hair long or short. Skin good or bad.
Us…
Us… girls and women with our skin dark as the night, every shade of brown, glowing like fresh-made caramel, or legs spindly like a spider, we are everything that is beautiful on this earth.
And *you…* you the prettiest of them all because you are *my* girl.
And your mother…

MAVIS *stands and struts in an exaggerated manner around the room – wiggling and dancing –*

Your mother can still turn heads...
My crown invisible but it there...

MAVIS *adjusts an imaginary crown on her head –*

And like any queen I can do anything I want!

You remember if you come from a queen then you must be a...

PRINCESS. A princess!

PRINCESS *starts to copy her mother's exaggerated posing around the room –*

MAVIS. So you take that pretty and you never let anyone tell you what or who you can be.
You free to be *anything*.
That freedom.
You never ever forget you have that freedom Princess.
So many princesses before you fight for our right to that freedom.
In here.
Up there.
It all yours.
You hear me Princess?

PRINCESS. Mummy you think I can win the beauty pageant and have ice cream?

MAVIS. Yes! And if anyone ever try to tell you any different you just show them your crown!

But ice cream will have to wait until Margot takes you to that den of sin Weston-super-Mare.

PRINCESS *hugs her mother tighter than she has ever hugged her before that day –*

Dance for me my little Princess...

PRINCESS *dances and as she does the room comes alive –*

MAVIS *watches her daughter with joy –*

WENDELL enters.
He is looking clean, smart and sober. He holds out his hand for MAVIS –
MAVIS *takes his hand –*
They dance – together – joyfully –

WENDELL JUNIOR *and* LORNA *enter. He is also dressed smartly wearing a sharp suit –*

Junior!

WENDELL. My son!

MAVIS. The James family going to celebrate this win today!
Into the sunshine.
Into the streets.
We all going out there to stand with our people.

WENDELL JUNIOR. Wait! Let me take a picture of us. All of us...

WENDELL JUNIOR *picks up his camera –*

PRINCESS *arranges the family for the photograph –*
She stands proudly in the middle holding her sister's hand –

A big flash envelopes the room –

Beat.

MAVIS. Come!

'*Di hotta di battle, di sweeta di victory!*'

FAMILY. Di hotta di battle, di sweeta di victory!

The family walk out of the room – except for PRINCESS *who stands centre –*

PRINCESS. This is just as I dreamt it...

All fruits ripe.

PRINCESS *laughs and exits – towards the sunshine outside, head held high, knowing that just for this one day, they won –*

Beat.

Radio crackles back on –

VOICE-OVER. *Breaking news! Today it was decided that the colour bar on Bristol buses is over. The company has already promised to interview ten coloured men who had previously applied for positions on the bus. The lead campaigner of the bus boycott Paul Stephenson of the West Indian Development Council said today –*

'Bristol coloured immigrants are grateful to the many Bristolians who gave support and sympathy in their struggle against racial discrimination.'

Scene Six

St Agnes, Bristol. September 1963.

PRINCESS *waits with her ear to* WENDELL JUNIOR*'s bedroom door. She is dressed in a swimsuit with a makeshift cloak.*

PRINCESS. Come out!
    Come out!

Beat.

You want me to help you?

The door opens –

WENDELL *appears – he is wearing make-up and has a skirt over his trousers – a shawl around his shoulders, and a makeshift headdress/turban –*

PRINCESS *claps excitedly.*

Daddy! Daddy you really look like a real woman...

PRINCESS *circles* WENDELL, *admiring her handiwork –*

WENDELL. Yuh better not tell any body 'bout dis.
    Yuh hear?

WENDELL *catches a glimpse of himself in a mirror –*

Lord! Give mi strength!

PRINCESS *pulls* WENDELL *by the arm –*

PRINCESS. Come on then.
Let's go.

PRINCESS *points to the door of the cupboard room –*

WENDELL. In dere?

Okay.

PRINCESS *and* WENDELL *walk into the cupboard hand in hand –*

The cupboard room is now bigger than it ever looked. The pageantry starts slowly –

WENDELL *stands speechless –*

PRINCESS. I told you Daddy.
I told you it was just like a pageant.

WENDELL. Yes yuh did.

Yuh do dis?
Mi never in mi life see any ting like dis Princess…

WENDELL *looks up – around him –*

So what do wi do now?

PRINCESS. You have to crown me the winner.

First you have to put the crown on my head…

WENDELL. I see. Every princess need to be crowned far true.

PRINCESS *jumps with joy –*
She searches a box until she pulls out the crown of the most wonderful sparkles –

PRINCESS. Then you have to say it like this…

'*Ladies and gentlemen, I present to you the winner of the year's Weston-super-Mare Beauties of the West Contest, Miss Princess James.*'

WENDELL. Juss like dat?

WENDELL *gently places the crown on* PRINCESS*'s head –*

PRINCESS. And now watch everything beautiful in the world
come alive…

*The room explodes into a world of pageantry – scenes of
people jumping into a swimming pool, Union Jacks, music
and fireworks – fill the room – and as* PRINCESS *watches
her world come to life, for the first time she imagines a
pageant where all the beauty queens look like her.*

*And as if the room knows just what she is thinking, a line of
the most beautiful Black women of all sizes and nations
appear before her. A line – a parade of women dressed in the
finest gowns, with the most coiffured hair, assemble around*
PRINCESS.

PRINCESS *puts on her sash and her crown, stands right in
the middle of the line and takes a bow with her fellow
queens.*

The End.

A Nick Hern Book

Princess & The Hustler first published in Great Britain in 2019 as a paperback original by Nick Hern Books Limited, The Glasshouse, 49a Goldhawk Road, London W12 8QP, in association with Eclipse Theatre Company, Bristol Old Vic and Hull Truck Theatre

Reprinted 2023

Princess & The Hustler copyright © 2019 Chinonyerem Odimba

Chinonyerem Odimba has asserted her right to be identified as the author of this work

Cover illustration by Cressida Djambov

Designed and typeset by Nick Hern Books, London
Printed in Great Britain by Mimeo Ltd, Huntingdon, Cambridgeshire PE29 6XX

ISBN 978 1 84842 827 0

A CIP catalogue record for this book is available from the British Library

CAUTION All rights whatsoever in this play are strictly reserved. Requests to reproduce the text in whole or in part should be addressed to the publisher.

Amateur Performing Rights Applications for performance, including readings and excerpts, by amateurs in English should be addressed to the Performing Rights Manager, Nick Hern Books, The Glasshouse, 49a Goldhawk Road, London W12 8QP, *tel* +44 (0)20 8749 4953, *email* rights@nickhernbooks.co.uk, except as follows:

Australia: ORiGiN Theatrical, Level 1, 213 Clarence Street, Sydney NSW 2000, *tel* +61 (2) 8514 5201, *email* enquiries@originmusic.com.au, *web* www.origintheatrical.com.au

New Zealand: Play Bureau, 20 Rua Street, Mangapapa, Gisborne, 4010, *tel* +64 21 258 3998, *email* info@playbureau.com

United States of America and Canada: The Agency (London) Ltd, see details below

Professional Performing Rights Applications for performance by professionals in any medium and in any language throughout the world (and amateur and stock performances in the United States of America and Canada) should be addressed to The Agency (London) Ltd, 24 Pottery Lane, Holland Park, London W11 4LZ, *fax* +44 (0)20 7727 9037, *email* info@theagency.co.uk

No performance of any kind may be given unless a licence has been obtained. Applications should be made before rehearsals begin. Publication of this play does not necessarily indicate its availability for amateur performance.

www.nickhernbooks.co.uk

facebook.com/nickhernbooks

twitter.com/nickhernbooks